Next Places
Seeing Yourself; Seeking Your Future

Next Places

Seeing Yourself; Seeking Your Future

Harvey Sarles

SYREN BOOK COMPANY
MINNEAPOLIS

Most Syren Books are available at special quantity discounts for
bulk purchases for sales promotions, premiums, fund-raising, and
educational needs. For details, write

Syren Book Company
Special Sales Department
5120 Cedar Lake Road
Minneapolis, MN 55416

Published by
Syren Book Company
5120 Cedar Lake Road
Minneapolis, MN 55416

Printed in the United States of America on acid-free paper

ISBN-13: 978-0-929636-57-3
ISBN-10: 0-929636-57-0
LCCN 2005938107

Cover design by Kyle G. Hunter
Book design by Wendy Holdman

To order additional copies of this book see the form
at the back of this book or go to www.itascabooks.com

Contents

III. Being-as-Extrinsic

IV. Becoming

V. The Study of Character

Frontispiece

Why is it, I have wondered, that whereas authors, poets, et al. in earlier eras produced their most important works in their later years, it is characteristic of our age to begin with the climax, also a distrust of life; thus almost everyone considers quitting early, a professor for a few years, a poet for a few years, an actor a few years, etc.—in short, as if the tasks were not enough for a whole life.

I think it can be explained this way, that instead of being character tasks, all tasks have become virtuosity tasks. This is why they are not enough. The ability to express the highest, to understand the highest, to present it, etc., can be achieved before thirty. But to do it—that changes everything and gives one a task large enough for the longest life.

But this is not what they want. They want to scintillate with virtuosity—and sneak away from character. This is why they turn aside. . . .

S. Kierkegaard, *Journal* #4475 (1851)

I

My Self and Myself

All the muscles of his face paralyzed to such a point that afterward it was hard for him to get rid of that mask of fear and terror.

M. A. Asturias, *Mulata*

The Essential Character

Looking at the photographs which were taken of that
    person who I am
who I call ... Myself
I see an identifiable person: Me.

I was and I am
each yesterday; every now.

How have I changed: which visages gone,
which remain?
Do I see
the same person I am, now?

Who was; who now?
Where will the next place be?
How will I get there?
How will I know
I have arrived?

What lost
given up, gained
... what cost?
... benefit?

On Losing Time

Perhaps it is, mostly, a question of age and of aging, but it is difficult to account for the past ten years or so. Somewhere, somehow, time got lost.

This is not true in any clear sense.
We can recover many senses of how we got here. The house got repaired, the children grew up; we went here and there, dogs appeared, friends materialized and did not. Yet in some deeply important sense, we lost time. Does everyone always lose time?

Do we want an accounting, a calendar of events that can be reconstructed from the sheaves of torn-off days? Will a schedule help?

It is as if we are visitors, new in town, finding our ways around, and ready to take leave in just a few days. Be analytic! Watch your watching.

And lose time?

How do we locate the character that lost time?

How do we note now that our time has been lost?

Is there something to do?

Vision Quests

There are: places, nations, cultures, times
where youth is directed toward a search for some
    essential being . . .
vocation, calling, vision.

Future portrayed, choices to be made early.
Search for the true way in life, to be discovered,
to be told by some force.
Knowledge? Power?

Once made, once the mantle of that vision is tried,
    worn,
become the extended version of self,
it is who one is, who you are.
You of past, you of future.
An anchorage, a place to be, to return to.
A quiet place in a changing world.

That vision: may turn sour, static. Long ago.
That vision: a source of power, energy, motivation,
    was and is not now.
That vision may cripple.

A vision may cripple in its finality which endures.
A decision made in youth.
That vision may yet determine today, updated or not.

A faith in youth-full good taste?
Now? What?

A vision that enables is
a model, a mold
an against-which
to measure what is now.

Which visions contain the space for approaching
    times?

Being as Being-Not

To some extent, who we are is about who we are-not.
not-like: some particular person
not-having: some particular traits.

We juxtapose our selves with others: being human is
    not-being an eagle, tiger, a mouse, a bumblebee.
who we are: moot, ambiguous
who we are-not: bounded clearly

Being-not has two phases: passive; active.
Passive: to not-be . . . a horse, a deer.
Different, they are, from us, but similar as well.
On the surface, we dismiss any kinship, but
carry some reservoir of being similar, of being-not,
    a horse or deer.
We exclude them yet retain them, those attributes of
being-not as potent forces in our lives.
an occasional dissonance in constructing a positive
    sense of life,
the objects of being-not remain; but shadowy,
    indistinct.

Active: we may choose to not-be someone, some
    thing.
We distinguish our selves, positively, clearly,
    knowingly.

Here we focus on particular features of not-being,
    to analyze, clarify.
we are, actively: not-evil, not-like some person,
    not a . . .

However, being as being-not entails various life traps.
we define ourselves negatively, not-being many others.

The strategies for not-being are critical in formulating
our positive characters, lest we remain in the limbo of
not-being many others,
but of being no one in particular.

Living like God

Kierkegaard said that it was impossible to be a real
    Christian . . . in a Christian world.
To be Christian is to be opposed: in opposition to
    whatever is a majority view.
Instead of being Christ's disciples, we should live like
    Christ.
Be Christlike in the experiencing of having to live
    like Christ lived (with translation to the present);
    having to do what Christ had to do;
and doing it.

Living as a Christian is either too easy,
or there is no possibility of being a Christian
in a world full of disciples, but not practitioners.
We change from Being, into thinking about Being,
if mere disciples.

Kierkegaard calls this a shift from ethics to aesthetics.
We become, aesthetically, followers who tell our
    selves
that we believe, thus we are.

The problem remains:
Do we continue to believe what we tell our selves we
    believe?

The Necessary Self

What is there of me that I have to have, in order to continue to be me;
to be that character who I am?

How much, of what sorts, can I yield without fragmenting, still being able to re-sort; and to rediscover those parts that are essential?

How can I retain the yolk and the white, while the world—the others—snip off the cracked particles of my Humpty-Dumpty shell?

Am I doomed, forever to be sorting the shards of life, or is there someplace else to be?

Where am I?
I am you, me, my past, a now, a now and then, an again.
Where am I?

Let me tell you who I am! Really. Who I am, really.
I am the person behind the front, the one who watches the appearance of my face in the mirrors of glass and of flesh, surprised at what you see, and at what I see.
Those are me, all right. I don't deny it. But it is not me, exactly.

Dodging, I am dodging.
Don't I know? Is there no me?

Look here! I know who I am.
As father, I am steady, trying to grow as my children,
as their father.

As teacher, I take on all of what it means to be their
teacher.

As husband,
I try to love myself half as much as you, and twice what
I dare.

Angry!
I love anger, especially my own.
Almost as much as I love the weather. Are they related?

Justice, I love the most. The justice in myself.

This is where it comes down, close to me.
That one I am, and the person I most need,
and can find most consistently;
by whom I justify my self to myself.

I am what and who I know how to love—in my self.

Being and Moving On

The immense difficulty in living,
is in maintaining integrity in my being
whilst being able to live in the present and for the
    future.

To maintain integrity in terms of some vision of self,
is not difficult.
I have merely to suspend present observation and
    judgment;
To bend interpretation in the direction of what and
    who (I) was.

Others?
Do they not tell me what is, now?

What is my view of others within this interpretative
    stasis?
Holding on to prior solutions to prior questions,
Others
become, remain
what we believed they were;
what we believed they were, at about the time
when a vision-of-self became firmly engrained.

The cost?
I have to deny, or to remake

the present/future in terms of this older,
yet younger,
version of myself in the world.

In rather odd senses,
I am at war with my own history!

History versus My Next Places

The constant confusion between:
what was,
what is
In my own life and in some larger world.

How I got here, was caused by
my personal relations,
by life's chances, accidents, purposes;
what I am because of what I did,
what was shown me, forced upon me,
what enticed me;
an urge
to become, to be disciplined, to be free,
to perceive myself and others,
myself-as-others.

My language, mine?
an accident of some others' time;
of their situation perceived by some predecessors
whose history is ended except in a few fleeting
    memories . . .
and as my life's perceptions and certain realities?

Where then do I search for the roots of my
    perceptions?

Where do I find, then, the apologetics for action,
now, and toward the future?

Which are useful?
Toward . . . ?

Perspectival Character

There are many aspects of Character; of any person's character. What we see as observers of others or of self, depends to a great extent on our perspectives. We see more detail with experience, but what we note depends also on what we have decided to not see, how often we count, and what we are looking for—both internally to self and to the observable situation.

In teaching, for example, I tend to look for (and to see) those aspects of students' characters that I know how to work on, or change; or those that scare me. All aspects of anyone's character are not apparent in any given sense, or situation.

On the other hand, all the aspects of my own character are also not accessible, even to my self. And they are subject to change, to context, to the vicissitudes of feelings, weak and strong. There always seem to be surprises, at least for those of us whose decisions about our own character were not made firmly at an early age. In this sense, it is difficult to be sure that there is a fixed or continuous sense of character that exists to be studied.

Yet most of us have a firm sense of our own continuity: of certain features of our being, of likely responses to certain sorts of situations, of analysis, of . . . how we'd like our character to be observed and considered. This is part of what we know and who we are.

The temptation is that we abstract and list what is properly dynamic, ongoing towards the future; that we make a reasoned analysis of *some* times into a recipe for *all* times. The danger is that we believe that what worked and works still, will always . . .

Where are those perspectives by which we can tell ourselves when it is a new time for us: a time to move on, to become?

The Handicapped Character

It has never, not even for one second in all this time, ever (never) left my mind that I have only one eye. In my case, the realization was easy: one moment I saw; the next was a hurt, blood, no more left side of my face as a locus, a placeness from which to look out. Empty, it is, in many senses. My left side seems to end at the bridge of my nose. It no longer confuses me very much, if it ever did. It never stopped me from doing very much. I am still active, jogging, even playing squash in a white-walled room. Not even a broken racquet. My remaining confusion is that I appear fairly ordinary, and no one else remembers. Just me.

I have some friends who are also handicapped characters: one almost blind, the other whose right hand doesn't work properly. The hand took a long, long time to discover. The blindness, encroached and denied, angrily rejected self and the world, finally acceded to. Being those bodies, they are what they are, and it is neither easy nor straightforward to come to the realization that they are ... special?

For those handicapped characters whose problem or deformity is obvious to others, it is the world that notes and remembers—but in ways that differ from those the handicapped carry in their internal imagery of self and appearance.

For us handicapped characters whose problem is

not obvious nor remembered, it is only my self which carries the image of being: different, special. How can anyone realize, understand, use such differences towards the future?

Does ordinary living, after some time, become its own handicap?

The Foreseeable Future

Optimist/Pessimist ... think differently; but in strange ways which depend on the nature of how long each sees as the foreseeable future.

True optimism is possible only through the acceptance of the deepest pessimism, because we must possess the freedom to continue to be, in the worst of circumstances. Optimism is thus often dour, and confused with a critical pessimism.

The pessimist yet goes on, the world outlook in a constancy of decline, with occasional exaggerated dips. History is rewritten on the side of "nay." Each today is less than yesterday, what was expected, and the world is evened out. Yet the pessimist goes on. Whatever is, is somehow necessary.

These states of being vary as well with the scope of personal horizons: How far away is our effective outside; does it impinge on thinking? Who will cause us to change in ways we imagine to be undesirable; how will it come about? How do we frame that imagination and phrase the trajectory on which we travel? Does it come from inside, somehow, or from external focus? Are we active actors?

What if ... ? What if ... ?—goes both ways, because it is those who ask this question who will see the conjunction and split.

What is the worst that can happen? The pessimist's

path leads slowly to its answer. The optimist quickly sees his or her doom, accepts it, and moves on ... in case it doesn't come to be.

Optimists are often melancholic as the immediacy falls short of what could be; the pessimist expects little and often gets more. It is thus often easier to sustain an active pessimism.

The optimist-pessimist approach to life is only sometimes paradoxical; as certain moments in one's personal life and the life of the world are truly fragile and in various degrees of disjointed suspension. What is often confused is a smiling countenance and a vice-grip jaw, with optimism and pessimism. But the paradox is rare in life, and not usually characterological.

The puzzle is how to see, critically, the foreseeable future. How far can it extend, in what directions? How do we see ourselves upon its paths? What will enable and lengthen it; what will foreshorten and block its realization? What seeing forward may become activated?

The Ontological Shift

From metaphysics to ontology::
from being to becoming . . .

Lessons garnered from the women who having
    grown up,
wanted,
needed,
to alter their beings and their perceptions.

Growing Older

How can I continue; keep becoming? Who is there to study; to study with? Most of those I know seem to have quit. They live within their memories, of golden days, the halcyon days of yore—when they found their greatest successes. They live on, no longer becoming, but having been and being still. Out of habit, perhaps. The present past, the past present . . .

Perhaps, angry. To have discovered that they live, that life is time, that living is its own history. To deny that, to wish away the future, thus to destroy each present as if it were created from what would have been. To wish, oh to wish that what was, still is. The strength for each new day derived from what was. No more becoming. And a being which was, but which is not, now.

But to become, each day should be more, more difficult, more. Each previous day got me here. Don't I know more? Can't I think better, wider, more clearly? It isn't a matter of being capable, but of the myriad strands of history wandering in to crowd out the necessity of moving on. Is it a loss of hope: the attacks of my own failings and failures cannonading each present? It is hurt, pain; the aches I have learned to protect against rather than to live (with)?

But being is no longer sufficient. I must become. And in becoming, I must study the nature of me as the character which remains in the world, while still being the character whom I can say—each new day—that I wanted to be.

—and to become.

On Being God

Looking for guarantees that if we live right, think clearly, love others, there will be heaven in heaven; and on earth. Is this a story; is it the truth? Feelings inspired, the pen glides across the page pulled by ... the hand of God?

How many are we—you and I? Perspectives we live aplenty. Isn't this an aspect of character not only to be god-like but so like God, to be?

But what of us is the god-person of each present? Do we want to be more than we are to ourselves: by mere belief, by wishing that the part of us which transcends is divine? And where does that leave us that we call our selves? Should the divine in us join rather than divide? Where is the god of each moment?

Can we still live life? Does life have its own terms? When do they apply?

How do we apply?

Counteracting Addictions

A friend has become an alcoholic. Which is to say that he has, with alcohol, taken himself to dangerous scenes, self-destructive, being here only through some grace or luck, or within another sort of knowledge that somehow controls in blacks and blanks. And we were asked to help commit him; to be placed in a place beyond his control, his leaving not his to say.

Why an alcoholic? Why does he imbibe booze to bomb beyond everywhere else?

In one sense it is an attempt to alter himself, to become another him, or someone else indeed. Yet who is to say which is truly him. He runs and runs, and runs . . . As he ages he goes beyond to run the marathon, twenty-six miles. Also an alteration of self, the self and character-as-jogger is not an experience, a beingness that is, for anyone who has not done it.

Is it how he feels each day? He says he is a disappointed person. What did he expect; imagine that this is less than? Are the running and the alcohol ways to manage disappointment; a good thing to do, an effort . . . a way of being?

In all of this complicated time of grief, my sense of being, my reason for being is challenged deeply. Life, living, incessantly fragile.

Can we accept this fragility, and use it toward tomorrow. Or must we destroy any concept of our next places, so we may protect our imaginations each today?

Nostalgia

The historical thinker's version of the "grass-is-greener" syndrome. Being historical thinkers, each of us has a weak theory of the present. To have an experience, even to plan to engage in that event, is to prepare for the future in which we can embellish and relish what is mundane as it happens; each present become food for future fantasies.

All that is, happens in the imagination; redoing the past to recreate it, to love it as a form of self-love; a concentration on getting here, with little note given to where or what we are, right now.

To whatever extent politics is present-process, nostalgia is either apolitical or a study of what was; not merely as it happened, but to enhance its memory. If done to perfection, the Golden Age is done. The present is a pale imitation; what is going on right now is probably unimportant. And probably, nothing can be done about it. At one extreme, life is no more than its own memorized study: removed and remote from living.

Other nostalgias: The perfect picnic—the historical thinkers who, always seeking the perfect moment in the perfect place, cannot ever find it because it has already changed by the time we get there. Or we cannot wait. The theoreticians—who, having a captive audience, play out in each present a story derived from a theory about what would happen, and it does, and it may—or it may not—have anything to do with the current situation.

Must nostalgia crowd out today?

Tomorrow?

The Malcontent

Why shouldn't I be angry? The world is full of so much ... hate, poverty, shit, blaming, power-hunger, vanity, all the seven deadly sins grown into branches, to their tips a billion times over. Selfish, blaming, justifying ... Their fault, not mine; not mine any more than theirs—feeds the contentiousness, simmers into a constant state of well-doneness, of ripeness with no pickers, no eaters, no maturity of being or of place.

The gnawing problem of self is a self-justification that works in each present but does not nourish itself as a remake of vengeance and retribution; of hate that becomes, anew, an involution of itself. The past become present in which the external characters of my formation become my own history, and accusing them has become the damnation of my self. This is the trap of the malcontent!

The reward of the malcontent is prophecy (which is its own trap)!

Boxes (1)

A young Marxist wants to know if there is work in her future as an academic (does not want to hear that there isn't). She is convinced the "establishment"—i.e., anyplace where she could potentially work—contains or is motivated by an ideology by which it manipulates and controls. She sees herself as an informed agent who will change the system and, simultaneously, is frightened of becoming that which she is committed to change.

The structure, per se, is what determines the ideology, she thinks. So, by becoming its agent she is enmeshed in a turmoil that, she thinks, she must lose. Evidently, the will of the system is so strong and hers so weak that they must destroy each other or remain outside each other's purview.

So there is no job that she can possibly take except to become someone she hates.

(A wise Marxist will tell her that, in a capitalist society, a wise Marxist is a capitalist. Is she saying that she's too wise to be a wise Marxist?)

The Best-Motivated Self

On self-evaluation: "Self-evaluation is carried out between the poles of self-respect and self-contempt." It is important "for the community of mankind that man become self-satisfied." Yet some self-respect always remains: "He who despises himself still respects himself as a despiser" (Jaspers on Nietzsche).

As a Teacher, what I seek in your character is your best-motivated self. I study you in order to find the persona whom you can tell yourself, you like; the persona who is able to live with self, yet who wants to move on. The best-motivated self retains some sense of futurity and of progress toward seeking a self that will be more self-satisfying. And I teach towards confirming that possibility.

The self that is best-motivated requires an accounting of and for its self. This sort of self-evaluation is dynamic in the sense that judgment has much to do with prior expectations of what any present would be; or should be. It is much like the musician's third ear: imagining the correct tone, a most lovely sound—against which to compare what the musician actually plays in each moment. To a large extent, present and future depend on how one applies correctives, updates judgment, and lets go of errors . . . sufficiently.

The best-motivated self is also a problem in how I think others judge me. How do I come to a sense of who I am; can be?—to some extent from how my significant others tell/told me about life's possibilities; how the visions of my destiny were drawn. Whether I attempt to please, to placate, to deny, I do this largely within the logics and outlooks of how some others think I am, thought I would be, and judge themselves judging me.

How can one's best-motivated self rise to the future? How do I recreate in each next moment some meaningful notion of improvement, of progress, of moving beyond? Must I get stuck in the daily failures of being only as good as I was; or of falling short of each ultimate vision of what might have been? How does any notion of self-evaluation become protective and progressive, more than destructive of each present, thus of all futures?

Who is the character that I can be, whom I will not regret, whom others hope(d) I might become?

Progress

How can I be sure that I am moving on and ahead while moving in time, through space? Why bother to worry about it?

Is there a difference between progress and hope? Do I know I have done more or better or more difficult, or that I have done less but died a little less? What is wrong with giving up or giving in? Is hope sufficient, or do I have to struggle; and for what pay-off? Is living well sufficient incentive for itself?

Would I live harder or better if there were an ideal, a God-like being, to be like? And if I arrived there . . . ?

If I do not . . . ?

A Good Arrogance

I like arrogance; deserved arrogance. It requires an arrogance to move on; to be able to say that I am better than, and good enough to . . .

Not everyone can do what I do. I can do it. Rather, I am sufficiently arrogant to try. There are many who think they cannot, and who think I cannot. But here I am, trying. And trying to do it as well as it can be done. And I am good enough to . . .

Better, more capable than I was, do I lord it over my memories of my self? How can I do it well today without appreciating how I got here? Yet, the rub is, I must dismiss that past as somehow lesser. The trouble in the present is that my theories of my own history are at war. That is OK, except that they now threaten to destroy my present: whichever one wins. Must I upgrade, or downgrade my past, in order to be good enough to . . .

How much arrogance do I need in order to try a new endeavor that then fails? How can I distinguish the taste of attempt from the often bitter saliva of having tried, having it fail, licking my wounds, and still move on? How much failure, of what kinds, can a good arrogance sustain?

How can I keep my arrogance within bounds; and behaving?

Down Days

Melancholy; aches; hurts that radiate from all those things I have done wrong and badly, to the futility and meaninglessness that underlie and punctuate all the things which I tell myself are fine on the other days, the good days. But, yesterday . . .

Was a down day.

Insane, crazy? Do I accuse myself, or do others tell me that I am? I am alone, so lonely. The others? They do not truly love me. They don't even know me. No. Not now. Not today.

What light? Heavy. Momentary relief. And back into it again. Quality? A good life? Bah. Blah. Mistakes, mistakes. Is there any longer a what could have been? Too long ago, too old. Why did I . . . ?

What am I doing here? How; why did I get here? Why didn't I know better? No longer, too long ago, to blame anyone else. My fault. My own fault. Stupid. Stupid. To have thought I was smart, to not have known what today is and would be. Not to be destroyed by others, but by myself. Oohhh!

Yesterday. Down. So far down . . .

Self-as-God

There must be more to myself than merely me. So much is inexplicable. So much that I thought I knew at some moment seems so unsure, so insufficient. I am a naïf, existing in a time that is no longer. And, I want, I want there to be more—is this all there is? Or I want there to be less—this is too much, too difficult. I teeter on the edge of craving total stability on the one side, unimaginable . . . on the other.

Can I construct another me, tentative at first, to explain, gradually, to become, thence to be, the hidden? It is me, yet not me. It could be others or the future; the once-was, or the other side of the mirror.

What is this other, this next? It is me, yet . . . And it is more. It is me, in dialogue with what might be, with some other-in-myself.

The problem is in creating the other in such ways that the dialogue remains interesting and productive: call it my self; call it my self-as-God.

Rites of Passage

I think I would like to be a knight. I think I would like to be something more ... than I am, or that I think I am. What am I? Hmm-m!

Down to Buckingham Palace with Alice, I ... hmm-m. How splendiferous, what pomp. Then I would know what I have come to be. But here, we no longer know how to celebrate a life. Perhaps we forget how to celebrate life ... living.

A twenty-five-year certificate, a gold watch in an era of a strong dollar ... was it loyalty? to what? to whom? Was it thoughtful, was it inertia? Did I love being it; sufficiently?

I'd like a team of horses, a big brass band booming out my name forever. Then I'd be a proper knight, something more, someone different. And I could start over; and really do it right.

Atonement

I have a friend who gets further and further into debt. A kind of buildup occurs over the year. I hardly dare intercept his pathways as the spring becomes summer, and the first signs of fall descend upon his spirit. Like a finite shell of steel, a blockbuster inside of a torpedo ready to explode with no place to go, and no way to get started. His nerve endings turn back upon themselves: a time to live, a time to be, a time to find his self congested into a massive mental traffic jam.

He tries: living within the present as the outer reaches of the past, turned back upon themselves, his theories of the universe mirror his theories of himself. Flashes of light refract into the turning of his year and jump off as they will, into the lives of others. They hurt, these flashes, but no more than the damage he inflicts on himself. Do we have to pay the price he must pay?

Could we but atone! Around the circle of being, come the Day on which the price can be paid for the bargain that is a life. A sense of peace, a kind of moral peak, a renewed ability to look forward. Could we all but atone!

Underground: Aboveboard

A current irony is that I appear to others to be a legitimate instance of what and who I am.

I look right, occupying a central aspect of the sort of character to which I pretend. What irony?—you might say: "How wonderful to look like what you are, if that is a good thing to be." And I can understand that.

Yet it is for me still, stylistics: externality. It calls—I am positive in some sense of self as an underground figure—it calls attention to their image of what I am, constantly filling in their love of their stereotypes, what they imagine. That is who they see, what they will remember.

My underground self, the mole-in-me that has sustained the real me, the Zarathustra-habit that is a cloak woven inward, forces me to subvert the character others see as me. The battle that has sustained me is at war with a destruction of self. That which was once false and superficial has become a reality that is flattering and self-seductive.

Can I remember the character I love while others respond to the character they love, in order to say what I must say, and what must be said?

II

My Self and Others

———•◦•———

"I'm a newspaperman," he said. "I don't write books, I don't write lyrical poetry, I write for goddamned newspapers. And newspapermen drink. And do you know why they drink? Because they have all those people in their heads, all those bodies, all those wives in the police stations with blood on their hands, all the sex maniacs with their eyes all crazy, all the burned babies at the fires, all the murdered cabdrivers with holes in the back of their heads. They drink so they don't have to sleep with the light on. They drink so they don't have to remember everything every time they sit down to write a story."

Pete Hamill, *Minneapolis Tribune*
(February 20, 1981)

Having Gotten Here

Well, here I am. But where is here, and how do I tell?

Looking back: have I turned out badly; well? Not so badly; not so well?

Am I reasonable version of what I planned; what I had hoped?

Am I moving on; becoming a reasonable version, tomorrow, of what I wish to have done, today?

Am I (still) sufficiently honest to be able to hear my own replies?

The Time Warp

We were visitors at a large eastern university some years ago. Located in a small city, it dominated the physical and mental landscape. It was what happened. Coming from an urban area that is seeking to be cosmopolitan with a vengeance, this visit was strangely out of time. The dominant mode of thinking, there, was formulated by a kind of endedness, perhaps a beginningness, which had occurred traumatically during the era of the mini civil rights revolution of the 1960s. While other people and places had used this time as an opportunity for reexamination, redistribution, and growth, this community seemed to see the world, still, through its vision of that particular time. Going there was, for us, a journey into our past, a time warp.

Events, people, conversations, habits of response like we had seen and been before, but not any longer. A rediscovery, a sense of having been here, but in our memories now, not in front of our eyes. Prediction seemed easy. A kind of updating for us, others played it all out, apparently for the first time. Life: a kind of television rerun.

Returning home through winter's deep, some 1,200 miles by automobile, we began to breathe differently. The trip's first day was easy, clear and cold. The next morning a cold fog set in, dawn broke bright approaching the Chicago lakescape. The mist cleared. We emerged into a newness, a sense for the present.

But where are we now, and when are they?

Whose present; whose ways of time?

The Observed

Knowing that we may be being observed affects the nature of our being. It is at once comforting and frightening.

In the tropics everyone lives out of doors. Constantly, there is the watchful vulture. We do not stay motionless for even one full minute without provoking a narrowing circle of interest, a mile or more above. A mere twitch, the great bird moves off to new searches. But the sense is so peculiar (to the nontropical person, at any rate), because the vulture seeks for death: simultaneously confirming infinite life-ness and life's finiteness. If transcendence emerges from dialectic, the vulture both causes and symbolizes. Perhaps it is even difficult not to become the watchful vulture; watching it watching us.

It is not so much being watched, as the awareness the watching arouses within us, that prompts a transcendent response. It is as if we become engaged with another version of . . . our selves?

We seem to be in some dynamic tension between what we feel in any moment, and what the observer sees, in that moment; between what is us, and what others see us as being.

We seem to be in some tension between what we feel and what we think the observer sees.

Is what we feel more real than the self observed? Is our sense of reality an outcome of this tension?

The Edges of One's Character

Boundaries: my character is bounded in several senses. But uncovering those areas of being is not easy, and it may be surprising even to my self.

My neighbors are currently building a new house on the lot next door. It was empty. Thus grass, light, color, and snow; unoccupied, mainly a city landscape that our kitchen window looked out upon. And our neighbors have an easement on what we thought was our driveway. They'll share part of it as access to their drive, when the house is built.

Surely, we didn't buy our house because it had an empty lot next door. And the question of an easement wouldn't have arisen if there already had been a shared driveway. Further, their home certainly will not devalue our property; it may even rise because of it.

Yet . . . it feels like an enormous impingement on my psyche. My deepest being is angry, hurt, vengeful. I have experienced the world greatly through anger, but this is as strong as anything that has ever happened.

Why? I feel that I don't even care deeply about having or owning a house. What is my investment? How much have I enclosed my character in the boundaries of house and yard? Evidently, a lot more than I had known. But I didn't know the nature and extent of this investment. I hardly even suspected. It is as if my entire world was being squeezed into ever-diminishing

Chinese boxes, and I, forced against my will, retreat to the next smaller. It feels as if there is no respite, no place to rest, no repose adequate to keep away those claustrophobic tendencies. How silly. But how true.

It is often difficult to know wherein we have made our mental deposits, how large our bankrolls, how susceptible to the right attack. It happens by twos and threes, then collapses by tens and twenties.

Isn't it the same with many features of our lives?

Self-as-Other

Who are we with respect to our selves-as-others? When we see someone we love, do we see merely that person? Do we see our version of that person: from the past; right now? Do we see that person as some version of our self, viewing? Love that person, or love that person within ourselves?

Perhaps my actual body (no mere image of self) somehow develops itself by incorporating an actual sense of significant others. Our mothers, our fathers, we have become to some extent. We are they, they are us . . . even in memory.

Perhaps my actual body is somehow developed or develops itself by incorporating an actual sense of significant others. I do not merely see or look at my mother or my father. I have become those persons to some degree, in some senses. Relationship is the stronger, the closer, the more we actualize these others.

Does this notion help in deepening understanding of Abraham's dilemma: "killing" versus "sacrificing" Isaac? Since the problem is (in) himself, does he find it easier if he believes he is sacrificing rather than killing? In either case he is doing something to himself-as-other (not to mention Isaac). What is the difference?

If a person kills—for whatever reason—then he destroys another. The focus is split clearly and cleanly between his self and that other.

If a person sacrifices, he has already created another aspect of his own being: God, mother, country, family, job. That aspect has its own place in his being. He sacrifices not merely the other, but also with respect to that "place" in his self, or for that extra persona that is simultaneously not himself and himself. It, like other significant persons, has its own beingness-in-ours. Yet it seems peculiarly powerful in its organizing force.

And those who are brutal, sadistic, punishing . . . do they hate the other-in-themselves? Do they attempt to find a purer self: to cleanse, or to destroy themselves-as-others?

Self-love? What can it mean? What does anyone know; how can I study the others-in-myself? How do I, whom do I, marry and sustain? How can anyone end a relationship and not be self-destructive?

Is the notion of self-as-other the foundation for us being political creatures?

On Being Beautiful

Some persons are thought to be especially attractive, even beautiful. Their appearance causes others to look at them, to dwell upon their bodies, faces, eyes, breasts, mouths, noses, skin ... to see some sense of excellence or perfection or wonderfulness, or ... themselves?

While it seems certain that the appearance of beauty is more about the observed than the observer, it nonetheless affects the person who is thought attractive. I am who I am, and they think I am beautiful; or, I am who I am, but they think I am ... beautiful?

There is some tension between what we see others seeing as our appearance and how we construct what we look like, from the inside. Our appearance is not fully ours. Not any firm possession, it belongs as well to others' envisaging us. We can only come to terms with how (we think) others see us; rather, with some of them, some of the time.

The binds are deep and difficult. How much to yield of our internal self, to others' pictures of that self? The question of "who I am," always close to the margins of our existence, is tempted to seek its solution in others' eyes. The temptation: to love in us only what others see and tell us that we are. If others see us as beautiful, we are left searching for that same image ... of our own selves.

Is there a necessary self, a self of some certain breadth or depth that can be found when necessary, depended upon to grow and to sustain? How large; for whom?

Can the vanity of our beauty be translated, be transformed into the more serious spaces in which we need to locate our selves? Against the day when we can no longer find the beauty that others see in us? Toward the days when we can find our own beauty?

What Works

Is there a "genuine" and a "spurious"—that which is true, pure; that which is anti and destructive? What is the pragmatic?

The first problem is in judging: from what notion of truth can I say what is now true and pure; what is anti-human or Satanic? Is present experience correct, can it be brought into line with what I think ought to be? The trouble: that a pure notion of truth often seems not to apply to today's experience. And it may not lend itself to thinking about becoming more, a character I would like to be, and to love, being.

Some days I don't have to ask these questions, and do not note the spurious forces within. They are managed and kept quiet, under control, a silence just below hearing. Occasionally they erupt and it is tempting to put them down as lesser, as belonging to some external force that wants to eat away and corrode the purer self I would love to think I am.

The dank and dark moods, I can call anti and destructive, but if life persists and they ebb and flow with better days, at least I can come to understand what is anti, to be what intersperses good times. And the judgment of what is genuine and what is not, may modify itself as I do the self-telling that leads toward futurity, as much as from the past. Stories of purity and truth in any simple or direct form may no longer apply, and what is genuine becomes what we are that we can both live with, and use to move on.

Or I may be weakened: the voices impinge. Wanting to ask the questions about truth, about purity, is driven by signals of deepening fear. Instead of looking within, I am tempted to assuage the fear and to accept whatever sort of answer suppresses those now nagging questions. In doing so, in burying the questions of today, will I lose the concept of tomorrow, or come to believe that hope will take care of itself? The illusion of each tomorrow infiltrates what was the reality of every today. No change is possible, and whatever is, is what works, no matter how . . . well or badly. It has to.

Judgment changes. What should be, is replaced by what is, as all roads become one; and the same. The lines blur and fade between what is Caesar's and what is God's. A theology for the good and the genuine is no longer distinguishable from what the theo-politician proclaims to be . . . good and genuine. A theocracy emerges in which everyone believes that everyone should believe the same. The methods for judgment differ radically from the plural world in which there are competing truths, in which each of us must update modes of self-judgment.

Can I find the strength to make my own judgments? Can I embrace my self; and life?

Ambivalence

Who I am; who am I?
Well, sort of this and that; more of, less of; well,
perhaps. Do only risks yield reality?
Who am I—not? So flexible that I must snap be-
fore I find my endings?
Who told me that I am, am not . . . ?
Just as we found skiing, the snow melted.

The Abdication of Strategy

Have some of us chosen not to choose? Were we defined by others, by our jobs or careers, or by our own histories, to the extent that we decided to forget to attend to our own developments? Where do we come down, then ... unwilling?

Were we told, did we believe, that there was no life after ... high school? Uphill till age ... thirteen, eighteen, twenty-five, forty, then a slow slide unto ... a daily loss of 10,000 neurons, slippery senescence, soft-headed, soft-muscled, soft- ...?

Was it because we expected maturity, a settling down; and ordinary living appeared to be all uphill, a struggle daily merely to hold what we hoped we had? A battle for turf, fame, riches won out over our claims to self? Peaked, peek-ed, piqued. No longer any promises, all promises had been kept ... or forgotten?

Did we pray for our souls, for our spirits, which we could no longer find? Were they in books, in rituals, in others' imaginations of what we were ... supposed to be? Wandering in the shadows of our time, we sought vision, we sought seeing. And it was someplace else, not within us. Not even the leaders of our selves, we had abdicated strategy. With no plan for tomorrow, we got up each day trying to remember who we were told we are ... told our selves ...

How do we rediscover today? Each day?

The Character-in-Opposition

. . . attempts to get its (my?) own way. Even if it has no way to begin with, the need to have its own way is often so strong that this brat-in-me will construct an argument (often an unimportant one) because what's important is winning, not what there is to win.

The best way to keep this under control is to give as much authority or actual control to the brat-self as it can endure. Here, I am likely to behave especially carefully, apparently because my natural move is to oppose the authority I just acceded to.

My character-in-opposition is often extensively a victim of the times, because it is shaped to a very large extent by extrinsic forces that I've perceived as political. I develop an anti- or a counter-character to some external thing or to some persons: a "them." If times change, I may be left high and dry; and if my earlier counter-view succeeds in the wider world, I may be left denying this self deeply.

The character-in-opposition, the brat-in-me, is developed by being an essential insider, but from a perceived position of lesser power; if not of weakness. The game is not necessarily winning, but of not-losing in particular ways. The strategy takes on moral suasion if I lose more as "they" gain more.

There are times-in-life and times-in-time when these aspects of self must emerge to ask hard questions, and to protect futurity.

What times are these?

The Edges of My Character!?

When, how do we make the sorts of decisions by which we set up the boundaries of character? If we are ever disturbed by a simple imposition on parts of our being, what else lies there, buried in the catacombs of character? Do these edges of character reside in some Freudian sense in an unconscious, or are they to be understood some other ways?

My edges seem to construct themselves by twos and threes, by very small increments or over a range of time that is outside, somehow, of the sense of being I carry as meaningful history. Isn't it like observing change in children? Look every day, we see sameness and continuity; look once a week, or once every month, and we are likely to note great differences. Our characters get packed while looking; but not seeing, or not counting. Becoming *is* being, perspectively, in small moments.

The edges of being can be likened to a linguistic dialect: a set of muscle habits that became habitual because they merely seemed the right and only thing to do at the time; rather, at many times, all of which collapsed in retrospect, into the way we talk ... and walk, and are. Each muscular accommodation places strictures on the ability to change, to learn the sounds of another language. Yet the original process occurred, apparently unbeknownst ... even to ourselves. And it occurred in ways that do not lend themselves to its undoing; only to its transcendence. Ways of talking—dialects—cannot be totally undone. They form a base of habitual movement that can be exceeded but not reformulated.

If the analogy is apt—dialect and character—then we may also see that the patterning of our tongues was not merely an internal event. It was not either, merely what it was: muscles that make sounds. The habits were not cultivated for themselves; they were internal events that, at each moment, appeared to be for or about something else. Like musical skills, we don't learn to finger or to bow a violin, we learn to play music.

But this doesn't mean that the habits are not deeply burnished into our being, becoming grounds of departure in terms of which personal boundaries are formulated . . . thence character: a set of muscular habits?!

Boxes (2)

A graduate student, fairly deep-thinking, was told he was brilliant: the best student to show up in many years. Eccentric, interesting; his own approach and ambience. Knowing more than the others, thinking quicker with more knowledge to draw upon, he began to believe he was extraordinarily good, and that his ability could spread everywhere. It could, he could, operate in all arenas in which his (*his*) subject matter was discussed.

He came into the larger world, where some of the other best students had found their own ways; where some had survived, and fewer had sustained the hopes and promises of their own youthful prodigy-prodigality. And the new best student tried to hawk his wares, well, but youthfully. That was OK, for the sustained knew the difficulties of growing, of being young; were neither destroyed nor destroyers. But they also knew that various sorts of humility, of humbling experiences had been their own way—perhaps the only way—and were not above teaching humility as one aspect of knowledge. They were demanding of themselves, and upon one another.

The student, having been deceived by praise, thought that he, too, had sustained, but did not understand that survival meant considerable adversity; far, far greater than he had imagined. He had gotten accustomed to using his knowledge and skills as bullying devices, having become convinced. Then he tried this with those who had been just like him. He remained too much in love with his prowess, and tried to engage his teachers in combat rather than learn greater techniques for engaging a larger world. Instead of reopening to more and greater thinking and knowing, he defended what he had and what he was; and faded into his own past as he misread the arenas in which he could no longer find himself.

Ego Size

Someone said to me that there was hardly enough room for the two of us in the same room. So I chose a bigger room. But I don't think it worked out ... at least for him.

Do persons have different-size egos; or do they have access to ways of using events and social structures to appear larger or smaller, or to occupy what space there is?

Do I "possess" an ego? Is it always there, waiting to express itself as the opportunity may arise? Do I have to do a constant and changing analysis of the scene in order to maintain a desired/proper ego size? Do I have several ego sizes—depending, perhaps, on the context and relationships in which I find my self?

I look at my left hand, which plays the violin fairly well: it looks like any ordinary left hand. Yet when the time comes, when it holds its proper instrument, it has a rather remarkable set of ideas of what to do to make music.

Are egos like that?

The Critic from Outside

But where is outside, and which outside? Often that critic is seen to be a crank, a complainer, a bitcher, pisser, and moaner, who must be jealous not to be inside? Why doesn't he be and do whatever he ought; whichever she is?

In a world of "ins" and "outs," the outs are perceived as other, and not criticizing, but speaking for the others; the outs. And they are not to be taken seriously. They don't want us to be better (the thinking goes), but to win, to get us to be (like) them. This is how it is because the world of ins/outs presumes that everyone is a lobbyist for her own position, for his own side.

How can I continue to be a critical thinker, taken seriously by others; and by my self?

Where do I reside: in; out?

Is this often an issue of context rather than contest?

At War with Our Selves

How many are we? Am I? And do I like all these aspects of myself? Do they enjoy each other? Are some of them despised or despicable—by others?

Who am I . . . not to like myself? Which is the I that dislikes the part that persists in spite of . . . ?

Am I invaded or constructed by external forces? Does Satan or do some angels own me and use me to fight epic battles of heaven and earth? Which is the I that observes the me that is zoned for war?

Or is it that I do things and feel things (the I that I tell myself I am) that I cannot explain, and which act badly just when I think they have gone away or have been purged or conquered . . . or overcome?

Or is this a story I tell myself to placate my yearnings, to guarantee failure, to plead weakness, to fall back on old habits, to return the clock to just past waking-up?

Here is the playground for martyrdom, where winning is losing, and the worst parts have to be developed sufficiently for the better parts to win a decent victory!

Lessons derived from watching our children growing up and seeing in them, at certain moments, exactly what we dislike in our own characters!

From the Margins

I came late to my profession. Twice was I other; twice was that wrong; twice was I mistaken; twice was I mis-taken.

And now I work within the gates, but find my self hovering about the edges, hopping upon the margins, never sure if I belong to my own be-longing. I am an academic and I am a critic, and wonder whence do I derive. Not an "out," not exactly an "in." Not an in . . . but not out; contained, but also containing.

To the real outside, I am what I am. I used to say: "I am an anthropologist: not a biologist, not a linguist, not a psychologist, not a . . ." What I said, if they listened, is what I am, what there is, and what is an anthropology. Now I say: "I am in the humanities, in literature, in cultural studies, a cultural critic . . ." Most don't ask what I am, but where I am; don't ask what that is, but seek to ascertain membership and status; to be polite, to call a halt to categorizing, to keep identity in some order.

Inside: a pariah, to be dismissed if possible; returned to the margins where speech is noise and ideas dance only on verges . . . to be dismissed if possible.

If not possible . . . ?

From the margins the horizon is clear. Here one can see what there is, as well as one's reflections within; without.

Traveling Light

What do I work for? Money, honor, success? Joy? The need to fill up and fill out each day? Looking for a place to look back from and say it was all ... all right?

Who manipulates those things, the rewards and payoff for good behavior and the translation of bad and all times into good times, or what is "good enough?"

Stand back. Look at myself in whose terms? Have I sold out? To my self? Who am I; for whom do I work? Rewards; character; not wanting to mess anymore with my memories?

Do I find myself being critical? Do I bitch and moan? Why not? Is what there is, what there can be? How much have I invested in being exactly who I am—and no more?

How much do I spend on what I have? Is what I have, who I am? How expensive am I? How much am I willing to pay? For what? Do I buy to maintain, to keep up; or toward ...?

Am I cheaper to rent; or to buy?

How much can I lose without being lost? How do I calculate how much I am worth? Who enters that calculation? Do I need an accountant to show me where my "shelters" lie? Will a bribe help?

Abandoning

It happens, often, that persons essentially abandon an interest or a direction in their work, life, thought.

Some do this because a direction no longer appears fruitful: it will lead them nowhere that they (now) understand as productive. Others find that interest (now) boring, have done whatever it is, sufficiently that it has become habit and ritualized: it is merely work and no longer "works" for them. Still others drift away, only to realize in some futurity either that they have changed or that what they do is no longer what does them; merely what they find themselves doing.

And many of the others do not define themselves as having or doing *work*, thus drifting to some external or extrinsic tune; all the while changing but not abandoning in any sense actively, in any positive way: what those who seek vocation call technicians. Technique, easy, young, virtuosity. The way to a career! Work is work for life, or life-work.

How can I move on, update, leaving what is earlier, younger, no longer me, without abandoning the self I am, and am to be?

Craving Crises

With sudden starts and spurts, intermixed with occasional moments of grace and repose, I am discovering that I want some crises to occur. Moreover, it seems a yearning; a yearning for a chance to do something: like searching for an intellectual jihad, a way to devote, even give my life some courageous terms. To have lived for . . . something, someone . . . to be important, a martyr to my own character!? The meanderings of middle age in search of a modern holy grail? Quite likely.

Life is a study, a curiosity, a preparation. Am I searching for entertainment, for theater? I am theater and entertainment . . . for small audiences. And the smallness, the selectivity is mostly of my own making. Should I take the show on the road? Will it play in Omaha, in Boston, Rome, Tokyo, Vladivostok, Nairobi?

Will there be appreciation; opposition; challenging directly; quiet, surly? Will it be shunted, responded to as something other, not whosever business it was calculated to argue? My worst fear: that all ideas have become so enveloped in bureaucratic and disciplinary cloth that mine cannot penetrate the mantle of ideation within any ideology.

And that is why I yearn for crisis. To burn this ideological coverlet, to lay bare the facts of existence, to be willing to see and listen to all the voices as *they* speak, and not by our selected and selective self-serving translations.

Terror of the Beast-in-Us

Much energy is spent in managing thoughts and feelings. Whatever they are like, the exercise of being-in-the-world often demands that we suppress, repress, shape, deny, forget, subjugate, conquer certain of these to the enhancement of others; at least to their public expression. Often this doesn't mean that they disappear from our being, but merely that the expression of them is framed in ways that others (and we-as-others) can deal with them/us, want to see us/them. To whatever extent they are suppressed, there is a reactive cost to pay, as they will pop out, awkwardly; for my self and for others.

If I have suppressed such feelings to the point of denial, I have in effect set up a virtual war within, in which the nature of the combatants remains somewhat unclear within my internal dialogues. It is often unclear, even, which side "I" ought to be on, and lifetimes are spent in figuring out where the "good" lies—whatever else there is being residual and "evil"—or vice versa. The "good" becomes definitional of what is human nature: what I tell my self I like about myself; the "evil" becomes the suppressed and denied, the enemy.

The problem of terror arises when the residual "evil" (the beast within) raises its ugly presentiment to my awareness, and actively threatens war. The Terror is that I have construed good and evil exactly incorrectly in my feelings, and that my life is worse than sham. I may then spend increasing energies fighting rearguard actions against what was formerly easy to suppress; the terror being that the best self ("good") will inevitably lose, unless . . . ; that I do not really exist as such, but only as a battleground of decreasing possibilities; that the will to carry on is increasingly self-destructive, and destructive of myself.

How can we extricate our selves, leave the battle, and retreat to another position in another war? Why . . . a war? Why not . . . ?

The Prophet

Woe is me! Woe are we! The world is on the verge. All is lost: my life, my love. What is next is nothing, or worse. Lament; repent.

The oil companies, the multinationals, the military, paramilitary, the loonies, crazies, the good gone wrong, the wrong becoming righteous, demonic follies ... they conspire. They want me and mine. Shall they not have me?

Ah! If only I were younger, stronger, more vigorous, full to brimming with the juices of life. Fewer juices, now; more excuses. What will be? No longer can I do anything.

What future? Downhill, a swift glide into the slavery of actuality. Maiming the edges of my mind. What to do? Nothing. Not one thing.

Who says that? Tomorrow? Not worse? How? Today is less than yesterday, and the day before was better than the day before that ... better, bah, blah?

Tomorrow? What fantasy do you spin, you Rumpelstiltskin of the mind? My beauty is gone. What I am is what I was. Tomorrow? Will there yet be tomorrow?

What are you doing to my mind? Are you trying to destroy me, to shock the fibers of my memory? How did I get here? What do you mean that I am wrong? I am. Am I not?

Today? There is something to do?

Why? What? How?

Character at War with My Self

The battle between: what happens & what has happened

    "   "   " : accepting myself & moving on

    "   "   " : theories of life; from life, from death

    "   "   " : models of beauty & processes of aging

    "   "   " : being good & doing well

    "   "   " : not-winning & not-losing

    "   "   " : my stories & my being

    "   "   " : preparing for work & performing

    "   "   " : necessary & destructive arrogance

The Dialectic of Self

Character is externally shaped—say the societologists. The self-willed self is nonexistent; how anyone is, is how you and I are defined from the outside, by others' perceptions and consequent treatment. Even if true, however, there is more.

At the very least, personal perceptions of being are heavily invested in being a particular way, being a particular sort of person, successful—even at being a failure. I must constantly come to terms with whether I am a decent, reasonable person in some sense that I can live ... with, regardless of how pathological, or how successful, I may appear.

The sense in which anyone may appear not to have a substantial inner character is also a statement about the regularity and constancy of her effective outside or audience. Example: in a bureaucratic setting, everyone is in many senses predefined as a role, a cog in the corporate machinery. A person is treated consistently as that persona, and comes to act as if she really is. In fact, fighting or opposing such an extrinsic definition of self places her over the edge of the role-defined self; she is seen as deviant, crazy, often incompetent. It is difficult to know, in such situations, whether a person is really crazy or incompetent, or that such statements are really about the nature of the boundaries and stereotypic elements of the role definitions and where in any stereotypy of envisionings a person is located.

In such situations it is difficult to know who anyone is and whether he is acceding to one's own definition of self, or to a definition that is extrinsic. There is a tension between these definitions: the greater the perceived payoff, the more likely everyone is to give in to the imposed definitions. This tension plays a large part in the formulation of character.

Possibly, in some deep sense, there is a personal self, mind, will, which is independent of all else; a particulate soul or spirit. But, in the formulation of character, it makes little difference whether the sense of self is really real or mythically real, as long as everyone operates in terms of its ongoing and effective reality.

All that is certainly knowable is that we have/are mythically real selves to the extent that we operate as if we are continuous, and will be the "same" person into the dim future. Then, we are who we are. The tension is between this notion of our own continuity and the extrinsic definitions in terms of which we are seen, considered, and treated.

The question of who and how to become next has to do with using this tension to move beyond present self-perceptions. A solution resides in being able to realize our own notions of success, and to become that realization, sufficiently.

III

Being-as-Extrinsic

———•—•—•———

Everybody's real to everyone else, but a
fantasy to herself/himself.

Janis (J.) Sarles

In Whose Terms

Let me see. What was I supposed to be?
Doctor, lawyer, preacher, teacher? Who knew?

Who knows? What was I told? What did I hear?
Did they know who I am?

Were they told? Who told them that I am?
What then. What now?

Who am I that I was told to be?
How do I tell myself that I am to be?

Development of Character

The process of becoming is some mix between the individual I, how others think I am; how they treat me and how I respond.

The individual is vague, unclear, hardly separable from its mother, even after birth. The emergence of self, the sense of who I am, is part of an interactive process in which others' pictures of me are well developed and elaborated in their range of possibilities. My being and behavior are interpreted within a worldview that is already ongoing; within a world that is well known as objects, processes, causes, and outcomes.

The onset of self, the beginning of will, the emergence of the person that I can see myself as being, is intertwined with talkness. Words that describe things enable me to describe my self as an I. I answer the queries of others asking who I am, by stating that I am, that I think, that I know them and the world they see; that I like them, am like them. Language, words, are ways to show that I exist, that I possess a will, a mind of my own. I have come to believe and to accept this appraisal, and am it. The individual I, comes to exist as a person, using an extrinsic definition of existence to believe in my own being.

At some points in life I began to study my own becoming in order to shape it in certain ways; and became the student of my own character. I stated my being and imagined my futurity, but listened as well to the voices of my self as others told me I am, and am to be.

In different ages and eras and settings, this study of becoming, of character, is more or less interesting.

Right now it has become compelling.

The Beginning of Character

From remarks on 5B, the obstetrics ward in the local hospital: how cute, pretty, yech-ch, whiny—too pointy a head (long delivery), good color. I'd like to take that one home; only a mother could . . .

What character? What's in a face? What do we see and project into that face? Already, by birth, we see futurity, a sort of person, a range of limited possibilities. (Do new infants "know" their external surfaces?)

This is the beginning of character—and what we see in that face may come to fit well, reasonably well, or hardly at all. But it is faces and facies that adults see, and facies and faces in terms of which we act (to a large extent), and the so-called freedom of being born-free is already circumscribed at the moment of being-born.

How the issue had arisen, in our family: on being with our grown-up daughter for an intensive few days, not having been with her for some months. She is really a very consistent character with the person I saw only fifteen minutes after her birth.

Um-hmm, says J., but "isn't she the same" might be saying that you see your own consistent image of her, which is the one that you saw in her when she was fifteen minutes new!?

Belonging and Loneliness

Who am I that I am like?

Am I like some other persons; do I identify my self as a member of some group, state, family, nation, church? Am I like them, like they say they are; am I one of them? Is this being-like-others, how I am; is it like I tell myself I am; that they tell me, I am? Are these the same?

When I say who I am like, is it because others have a picture of the world that is already too complicated, and in which each new I is a burden upon the crises of overload? Do I tell them that I am ... a ... because they demand it, because I think they demand it, or because I actually am ... a ... ?

Does anyone always belong? What is the contract? Do I always endure as ... a ... , or do I lose my own sense of being if I am no longer like ... a ... ? Is this what is loneliness? Am I truly alone, a-lone; or have I lost an aspect of what I thought I was ... like?

Do others say also that I am like them; or like what they are like? Do they do for me as I do for them? Would they, if I did? Do I do for them? Do they, for me? Do they, still? Do I, still?

If what I am like changes, what happens to me? Am I still like what I thought I was, or must I, too, change? If my family or corporation or church is no longer what it was, or even what I thought it would be—by now—

what is it that I am like? My memory? My imagination, from some past, of what today would be, but is not? Is loneliness, then, some dialogue between what I thought I belonged to and was like, and what I imagine is the case, today?

Why should my imagination make me hurt? Should I consult a doctor, a teacher? How do I go about consulting my self?

Temperament, Constitution, Character

What am I like, what are we like, *essentially?* Are we born with a destiny, predetermined, our characters and lives engraved in the blueprints of our being? Were we born well? Can we overcome tomorrow what we think we are, today?

To have a good temperament is to behave well or properly, by some notion of what virtue there is, and what virtues there are. But these vary in different places and times. Cleanliness next to godliness: of soul, of character, of hygiene? To have courage when there is none called for, is next to suicide. To show repose on a calm day, is banal. Is temperament a cast of mind, a permanence in gifts from our antecedents? Or is temperament a theory of being, an analysis of some universe and of my self within it? Is it continuous because it is; beyond knowledge and outside of control?

To have a good constitution is to be healthy and strong. Are the best the healthiest and the strongest? Are our judgments of what is best tempered or structured or framed by a pathologist's vision?

Can any of these be altered, studied, shaped? Do they require work, luck, habits of mind and of being?

The Universal Self

But why do you ask? Are we not sufficiently like one another, for: understanding, respect . . . ? If we are sufficiently alike, why is there any hate, wars? If each tomorrow is truly a new day, how can we relate at all; to one another or even to our past or future selves? Does each of us wander, alone and lonely, traipsing out the individual trajectories of our destiny, crossing paths only occasionally, with no true connections?

Destiny, Providence—did we begin alike? Are we all going in the same directions? Must we believe, accept a single story, in order to get wherever there is to go? Does it help to read the same story, recite the same words, if we read—all differently? If we are all the same, if we all want the same thing, why is there trouble?

Perhaps, as some say, life masks. The experiences of living paint the surfaces of our souls, appearing distinct to others and to our selves; the patina becomes real. How do we chip off that shell, how do we return to what we were . . . to be, what we supposed ourselves . . . to be?

Maybe we are damned. Damned merely by being. What can we do? Should we save? Ourselves; others? Whom do we have to destroy in order to save? Our selves; others?

How can we get past the myths of likeness and of unlikeness, to begin to talk, understand, respect others and our selves?

Clowns and Clones

Vocations, callings, provide a metaphor in terms of which character can concentrate and center itself. Or it may provide a definition of role or of character that we can use to avoid the struggles of becoming. Put on the mantle, and be!

Surely the clown is seen as, treated as, thought of as, a clown: a countenance painted each day. The clown's vision is really, deeply different from the vision of anyone else because the clown sees reflections in the mirrors of faces seeing . . . a clown.

Are we also clowns? Doctors, teachers, police? Is a vocation a way of being, or merely a way of being seen, of being regarded and treated? Surely it depends: on the viewer, on our experience; what we see. Perhaps it depends more on what is, but which we do not see, because of our mantles.

How can a physician see healthy people, when called upon constantly to treat sickness? How can a politician see persons, not merely interests and votes and constituencies? How can a bureaucrat . . . ? How can . . . ?

How does the wearing of the vocational mantle change through time and appearance? Does it fit better at some times rather than others? What happens when the act looks good, but feels bad?

How can I learn to see the self that others think they see in me; to love that self sufficiently; but not too much?

A Narrow Slice of Life

The world grown big in terms of numbers of persons. The need to reduce those numbers, to disattend to the complexity of each character, to remake persons into type, roles, sorts: teachers, doctors, preachers, managers, marketers; each sort assigned a limited response, appropriate to ... what anyone does, who she is, and how we are to deal. Experts, professionals, know-it-alls, models of being with the texture and density hidden from sight; gradually hiding from insight as we become the special person we chose and are assigned.

Success tends toward the technical as meaning is pushed to life's peripheries. The more knowledge we have, the less it seems we know. As we become expert, as good as good can be, our range of knowing condenses. The small details of our lives expand to fill life's thoughts, and become a veiled vision through which we interpret all we think there is, and all there seems to be.

How can I become more without becoming less?

Depersonalization

There are various ways by which we rob ourselves (and others) of any depth of meaning or breadth of being. Mere facts of size and scale force us to be: a student, an employee, a person who does such-and-such; a boss, a manager, a general, corporal, a believer, dissenter, a . . . some one. Some . . . one!

We create a *they::they* create an *us;* which is neither you nor I, except in odd moments.

I am what others claim I am, and no more. The *I,* I think my self to be, is a mirage. I am a product, increasingly, of my self.

Who am I really? I am some sort of product, some theory of how they imagine me and how they imagined I would be. I am a student of life's changes: told how to see, told what there is. I am a critic of them, of what they see as me, of what I think I am. The *they* I see: is it really their *they,* or the *they* that I create out of the wondering of who I am?

Out of what worldview did they see me and know me? Did they love me? Did they hate me? Did they rob me out of hate; out of love? Did they feed and sustain me? Hate? Love?

I am father, husband, teacher, person, neighbor . . . does that leave any me? Am I hidden? Will I be recognized when I find my self?

The Lady and the Harp

Yesterday (Palm Sunday) we performed Fauré's *Requiem* in the church upon the corner where I live.

There was a young harpist who soloed before and after. She played quite beautifully; our only non-amateur musician, a Minnesota mercenary. There is a way to grasp the playing of the harp that is plainly available to the observer: hand, fingers, wrists appear large moving in circles; dampening, plucking in a natural extension of the musician's body.

A four-year-old girl was in the first pew, watching intently; almost being-a-musician, she was that close. I met her eyes several times, and we winked in the kind of intimacy that meant we shared a special, almost sacred experience that nonmusicians were never, ever, privileged to explore and know.

After the concert, in the choir-orchestra room, one of the choir members—a woman who seemed to pray with a particular fervency—spoke with the little girl. "The harpist played like an angel," she said. "If you learn to play the harp, you'll have a head start," she concluded. "To heaven," I supposed. Life-existence only as a preparation for the hereafter. Life as a . . . how frightened for her soul. How does this orientation rule her life?

The same woman also drives the church bus. Is she safe to ride with? Does she know the difference?

The Structuring of Character

A church, for example, can create the idea of a nun/ priest, define it, embellish it and sustain it. But not always, and not for everyone.

We are emerging from a period in which this did not *work* for many persons (bright, attractive ... ?). Why did it cease to work; for whom? Why does it work, apparently so well in *ordinary* times? What are the limitations on the nature of character shaping by a theo-political organization? Are these ordinary times?

Certainly, there is a certain give-and-take. We give away certain aspects of character, partials of our freedom of self-definition, in order to participate more completely as that self which is defined and supported by the social structure. What do we give away? Is it a gain or loss? When?

We yield to a kind of mind-set of restricted possibilities: an entire range of being grouped into a single set to be juxtaposed with what anyone is. A dual thought structure is thus created. Where there might have been ten (or a thousand) such possibilities, there are now two: what I should be versus what I cannot be.

And in the drift of mind over time, each of those areas develops. We give away the *might have been* of possible development, running only a pair of thought modes. This is not to say that the elaboration of thinking within any two-part framework is simple-minded or nondeep. It is certainly restricted or restrictive.

Depending on the arena-of-being within which the juxtaposition is created (life-death, man-woman, change-continuity . . .), the metaphysics develops and elaborates. One side gains prominence in any particular era, the other fades. But the out-of-favor mode is nonetheless elaborated, since each is ultimately dependent for its boundaries on its implicit other. Life, that is, is full of paradox(es).

Even the emotions may be structured within a particular organizational definition. *Anger* is, for example, a statement about sin in some church contexts, thus an expression of the devil. It must be suppressed or redone so that its expression is denied. Persons who feel, experience anger, must somehow act as if they don't feel (like) that. Since most of us can become expert in denying and restructuring such feelings, we can read our bodily changes not as anger but as sin. If unsuccessful at repression we may interpret those feelings, those emotions, as an alien or opposing force within.

Some church structures support this and reward it by interpreting such denial as *goodness*. A church may thus be in the position of defining bodily states according to what it holds to be a theology. It may be that the nature of the theology or organization is essentially irrelevant to this process. But certain ones work better or more efficiently in particular settings and times.

What we gain in return is a kind of guarantee of existence. If we are successful in terms of some organizational definition, then we exist. If unsuccessful, we still exist; even as misfits. Everyone has a place. Such dualistic definition is inherently antinihilistic. It provides a location for beingness. We can find our selves here.

There is a difficulty with such definitions of self during periods of perceived change. During the past decades I have taught a number of ex-priests and ex-nuns, as well as would-be nuns and priests, whose existence was, early on, postulated and formed within the notion of the external ongoingness of the church structure. In effect, they had (already) yielded some important parts of their independent-able selves to an external church definition. When the church was no longer viable for them, they found (find) it difficult to construct sufficient integrity to sustain themselves. They are incomplete and weakened, much as a child whose parent has died, or the disciple whose mentor has fallen, and need a period of recovering as if from mourning.

But it doesn't seem to matter much whether the structure is a church or any organization in which we live a major part of life; e.g., corporation, university, business, firm, family, academic discipline, or culture.

Whenever it doesn't sustain . . . ?

The Job Description

There are many settings or situations in which there is a tension between who I imagine my self to be, and who I am said to be; or told to be. Within this dual/plural construction, the varieties of solution to who I am, can be tremendous; often I cannot get unstuck.

Consider a bureaucratic setting: a person is hired to fill a job description, the job described with reference to how someone imagined that job, or how some particular person was thought to have actually done it, or in terms of how it might fit/function in a corporate structure. In the job, in doing such a job, you may actually attempt to be that job description. As long as you principally are/do the structural job (e.g., bank teller, manager, nurse), then the tension is minimal. If, however, the dynamic aspects of conducting yourself are contradictory, out of place in a given setting, the tension between who you are and who you are supposed to be can be enormous.

There are many ways to handle or to resolve such tensions; so many that we could write a world history in their terms. But there are favorite sorts of adjustments. Different settings teach different techniques: adaptation, denial, dissent, waiting, martyrdom, sacrifice . . .

Each of us must work to deal with felt tensions. You and I can change. We can come to see situations differently, as well as being the passive compliant. How do we invent perspectives from which to study who we are as the setting defines us? Places of repose from which to view our own viewings?

How can we become, neither destroyed nor destroyer; become ... a person who sustains being one's self within the tensions of being others' invention?

The Architect

Sees the world as the space and place, constructed or not. The visual aesthetic is worked on in each moment, waking or sleeping until the aesthetic rules reality. Seeking for perfection, the observer diminishes. The ideal become the real, I fade into the background.

What is background; what frames; that which is below with respect to what is above; bounded or unbounded; in color, in blacks, grays? What seemed abstract becomes the tangible.

The architect's vision: not interrupted by persons or by humanity. Persons become cutouts; in color, in blacks, in grays? Shadows illuminate the spaces until the spaces, only, exist. As the cutout people fade, the persona of the architect-observer becomes abstracted, reduced to points of observation.

Where am I? When did I fail to appear?

The Visitor

She sits outside of us, watching, observing, remembering. The world constructed within the confined abstractions of life's exiles. How to maintain the proper and necessary distance without losing connections to the tentacles of otherness? How to stay outside, yet to know where home is, where ground resides?

Time stopped; for her, several times. The future, the present not blurred, but interpreted; conceived each next day as the world that would have been. There she sits at age five, seven, twelve ... Does each age have its distinct framework? A true romantic, life is never quite right. Her trick: to maintain the view that life is just slightly worse than it is. One eye seeing, the other looking to make each present into something lesser. She, the residuum, rises like fresh cream. Life; skim milk, necessary to keep her afloat.

Intense, an assault, always questioning, forever wondering and wandering in the freshened details of her mind. Thousands of people in myriad relations, like a sea of floating balloons, losing helium, seeming to drop. Each day, all get renewed, new breath, buoyed up into their proper places. Increasingly they are dead, but no matter. Her work: to pump them with life's air in memory; each new day to recreate them, thus herself watching; the visitor.

Energy

Finding ourselves in front of a Jamaican reggae band. They began to play. We in the midst of a thousand dancing bodies, moving variously but vigorously to the pulses of the steel drum amplified to fully fill an entire meadow. Twenty years younger, they all were entranced, captivated, given up to movement. Momentum, energized waves of sound, rolling out to us. We, too, had to move, to dance, to feel the music, to be it, to be at one in the midst of such a group. Excited, energized, moving.

What is this stuff, this energy? Eight hours rest, work, relaxation; food, loving; wearing down and wearing out

Rejuvenation: a searching for the foundation of a youth-full America? A crib-to-crypt accession to a senescent self.

Responsibility! They are all like gas-guzzling cars, emptying me, draining my tanks, laying bare the reservoirs of my self. But sometimes they give back. Must we be in a system of mutual drainage? Can I get and take, and not destroy? Do you know where there is some energy?

Can I teach you; can I heal you; can I help you? Or do I provide somehow the energy, the boost to will, to will yourself more?

The Critic from Within

Who gets heard? Who gets taken seriously as the critic, as the person who can say, "Yes" or "No" and make it stick? Most often it is one of us, our gang, the players of the game, who changes his mind, who is a turncoat practitioner. Most often, it is she whom we listen to, whom we hear.

Even if the ideas come from the outside, even if their inventor is the original mind, it is from the mouth of the illustrious insider that we take the new ideas; from whom we can hear them.

They are his: they are important because he says they are, and shows us why they are important, and what his thinking is.

Why we hear is because our thinking is hers, and hers ours, and we can follow from where we are to where she has gotten; in our terms.

Why that person—often a mere translator— becomes credited with the idea, has to do with facts of group identity. The critic from within becomes important, the ideas are heard as his, especially when that group possesses a good deal of prestige, and chooses to believe that ideas emanate from within ranks; if they are actual ideas.

How do we relisten: to attempt to hear what is there, and what there is without letting group identity dominate being?

Seeing What There Is

In our town there is a biggest building that reflects the sky and the weather, the dawning and the setting sun, the moods and frustrations of a city on the prairie. This biggest building, which reflects, so dominates the landscape that it fills many of the windows, looking out at our lives.

Some people, looking out, want to see forever, or as far as they possibly can. But the biggest building, which reflects the world between it and you and behind your head, is in the way. Instead of seeing out, you have to look back. It restricts, it shapes, it mirrors, it owns our views. "I hate that building," she says.

"Go closer," we suggested.

"And when you get up to it, walk inside. It is its own world, hovering over the street, slick, shiny, glassy. Inside, it vaults up several stories in a castle-like apparition, glass-topped; a real court. Everyone is here: the lawyers, the doers, the pimps and watchers and teachers and kids and visitors. It moves, together.

It is the hub of a city, peopled, bustling. Not merely filling the windows of our lives. But breathing. Then walk away; go back to your windows and tell us what you see."

"Does it still annoy; do you still hate it?"

The Now

For years I have wanted to make a career, carved as it were from the Great Calendar. Walking with a certain certitude, I knew "now" was; I just didn't have an actual grasp on exactly when it began or ended. As all philologists, I studied the forms: is, was, will be. But got stuck, as usual, in the interstices: the edges and boundaries and moments between. I had never been able to decide whether there is more freedom in between, or whether this position of some apparent repose allows me to decide not to decide, when I am.

Then I went abroad to a land of preliterate people. Before history, before time?—I wondered. But they, too, possessed time: with days, nights, the passing and passage of the sun, the moon, and stars. They knew birth, growth, marriage, death; and had rights and rites. They knew now, and then, and would be, as well as is, was, and will . . . be. They also had edges, which we wandered through. When is this?—I asked. They, too, shrugged.

Without watches, they were more precise. Without writing, with no charts, no books, they kept it all in memory. In each and every instant, their active histories were fuller by far than mine. Without books, life was nothing other, no more than everyone's mind-full imagination. And I learned from them, that what is, is what everyone thinks is; that everyone possesses a now, an experiential now; that time is not, except what we think it is; that we are it, create it and invent it; and live.

And so, as theorist of the present, I abandoned the study of is, was, and will be. Now I study persons' theories of the present, and am certain that I am now, closer to knowledge, placed within time, an aspect of its formulation; not outside; not merely being, but becoming.

IV

Becoming

———•—•———

There is really no occasion for despair:
our world can be computed even if it
doesn't exist.

Carl Becker, *The Heavenly City
of the Eighteenth-Century Philosophers*

Rabbi Ben Ezra

Grow old along with me!
The best is yet to be,
The last of life, for which the first was made:
Our times are in His hand
Who saith "A whole I planned,
Youth shows but half; trust God;
see all, nor be afraid!"

Robert Browning

Another Day

The labyrinths of life in which I might have been, contrasted with where I am ... And where to go?

Which tomorrows will I live? Which tomorrows will live as me?

How to get where I want? How to want where I might get?

Well, today is today. Life becomes no easier. When do we shift from life to living?

How do we live to know that we have been living?

What is living that we may know our worth?

Ensuring Futurity

In different times and places, the concept of a future may appear clear; or it may seem murky. How we decide today to live toward tomorrow often turns upon this perception.

If there is a written or known script, if we believe that our future is discernable, then we can study and work at this script as a model for what to become. The *Analects* of Confucius are like this: the ideal of venerable old age, the end toward which to aim a life, to direct a character; a way to stay upon.

In a scripted world, what life is, and what life is for, appear to be clear. This both presumes and creates a static society in which life is the road to old age; the path is direct. Each step leads to a next . . . and they add up to the kind of life-as-perfection—a Way—which Confucian-like schemes offer: there is a path; stay upon it; and . . .

Where change is an accepted fact of life, when the future is blurred, when the concept of maturity has faded into wonderment about the ongoingness, it is never clear how to act, how to gauge thoughts or deeds, what is moral or not. The entire question of morality, right and wrong, depends on some vision that seems external to being at any and every moment. Thus, it is that our pictures of God, of old age, usually include a constancy and consistency and continuity within which we always can find our place. Just now, however, it is as if being human is not sufficient; no longer enough.

At such times, when we are tempted to reinvent the external/eternal, it is important to seek out and to become yet-living teachers, interpreters; persons of experience who have grappled and grasped and groveled in the silts of time; who can do, who may tell us what there is; who may discern where we are.

In a changing society, it is necessary to have and to become characters who are able, still, to live in each present, toward some vision of future; teachers who ensure the future, guarantee and motivate the present. Here is a notion of progress; how and why there must be interpreters of all texts, and teachers toward all times . . . within this time of our living.

Forgiving

Who of us has earned the right to be forgiving? To forgive is to be *good enough* to have been wronged; or to be innocent. To forgive is to have been assaulted, to have sought vengeance, retribution and to have moved past needing to strike back. To forgive is not (merely) to forgive others, but to have moved to a place where we can forgive our own anger.

Much forgiving is false because few of us have earned the right to forgive. People who say they forgive—frequently—seem to have an exalted sense of who they are, an undeserved arrogance whose image is penetrated and punctured. For them it is easy to forgive. They need take on a mere mantle of holiness; the kind that is station and appearance and semblance. They can forgive without cost, cheaply.

From innocence: forgiveness takes much more. To have been roped in, to have been taken by those who had advantages of size, or age, or various dependencies. To forgive those who had power, sufficient to dwarf the previous relationship, to have accepted whatever happened, and to have placed it in perspectives. It is to have overcome an inferiority out of innocence, and to no longer savor innocence and the safety of not-knowing.

To forgive, is to forgive self and history, and to reformulate character by loving innocence; to use it, not to mourn it.

Inspiration/Curse

We had mounted an inspirational proverb on our refrigerator: "May you live in interesting times."

"How wonderful," we thought. "How nice to have a positive way of appreciating the times in which we live. Whether they are in some sense intrinsically interesting, or this is a way that can lead one to evaluate one's life and times in useful ways, remains moot. But we enjoy the concept as a kind of credo, which is positivistic and appreciative of whatever we experience, and a gathering of the good and of the rough times."

A young acquaintance was referring to the proverb as an ancient Chinese *curse*: "May you live in interesting times."

Crises of Nerve

A good deal of mature development concerns itself with smaller or larger crises of nerve. These are events in our lives that we ought, perhaps, to go at or about. In a crisis of nerve, we decide not to, for a variety of apparent reasons: not ready to, don't really want to . . . But, in aftersight, it has turned out that not doing some of these was more costly than we knew. Not having done some thing, we had gotten more frightened rather than more prepared, and finally incapable. Such are crises of nerve.

In teaching, for example, unless you abandon notes-to-teach-from about the time you are finally knowledgeable about your subject matter, then it appears that you are unlikely ever to do so. The opportunity was effectively lost. You are weakened, and this may transfer from the arena in which it occurred, to other aspects of life, possibly in ways that powerfully shape character.

It is difficult to say, precisely, what a crisis of nerve is, for any particular person, except in hindsight, because of differences among people. It may even be that some of us are never tested in such ways, or that we do not approach our lives such that crisis occasions can arise.

Problems occur in recognizing which sorts of situations are in fact (will turn out to have been) crises of nerve. If not prepared to do something, it is usually silly to pursue it to certain failure. But how are you to know? And to know how much the eventual cost will be?

Perhaps it is more important, in growing, to recognize early when such an occasion has been passed through, and to determine ways to overcome or to compensate for a loss resulting from a crisis of nerve.

In becoming, it is important to permit such occasions to arise: as they will, and how you will.

Intellectual Quitting Time

I thought that true intellectuals probe ideas, ask tough and difficult questions, pause, think anguish . . . But no! Most of those I know turn off at certain points, when the going gets tough, when their psychic ends get bared, twisted, and singed. Then their eyes show that certain glazed-over look. They turn soft behind their eyeballs and yell, "Foul!"

Who are these nine-to-five intellectuals, the global thinkers whose widening thoughts outstrip their life experience? Are they real thinkers, or are they paper intellectuals?

Whom do they yell "foul!" at? At the person who is the tougher question asker; the person with the wrong style; without the proper credentials?

I want to be able to think about who I am, who there is, and what there is, to be. I want questions, ever more difficult; not answers to problems that I have moved past. And I want them carved from today that I can still wonder them.

No. No stopping. No method. I want to think, clearly.

On Alienation

There is a notion that we moderns are separate from our native, natural, archetypal, primitive selves. Somehow we need to, want to, must return: but, to what?

Born into today: yet a sense lingers of some human essence whose personal recapture would provide a taste of satisfaction; of fulfillment, even of a destiny.

No doubt we are in some deep senses always removed from our selves. The common explanation is that of an inherent individual freedom that is impeded and restricted by the pressures and demands of society. The experience of being alienated: due to some strange war between individual and society in which we are all engaged. The proposed antidote: to return to ancient times; before society, before history.

Instead, it now appears that social living was always our way. It is that society which grants and defines our genuineness. We only discover or uncover a sense of self as others treat us as if we have/are continuous persons. We are engaged in some lifelong dialogues between what we are told is possible, the dances of each day which we live; who I am and was, who I am not and whoever I can/cannot be.

The antidote to the alienation, the sense of who I am not that I should be, is to develop a sense of being as becoming, as character; of a person whom I can be, continuous both with respect to the self I believe I am, and to the outside whom I regard as significant. Character: a form of self that is always unfolding; a perpetual study in self, but also always new.

Otherwise the present and future tend to be some reinvented illusion from our pasts. Who are we that we are not our selves? How do we find the aspects of us that are other; mend them, be them, or let them go?

Becoming-non-Becoming

Confucius tells about developing character as emulating the life of the ancient wise person. A mistake, I believe, is that the character of the already well-developed Great Person is often characterized to us as if it is directly understandable.

Each age (and each age in every time) will understand such portraiture differently. Any singular depiction of wisdom or greatness tends to become a peculiar dogma about greatness, not about living as it informs anyone's actual experience. It leaves almost no space for (self) discovery, and takes on all the trappings of a religion as it is virtually impossible to ever be a humanly Confucianist form of the Great Person. So it was and is tempting to set up rules that are claimed to be guaranteed to achieve the good life, according to . . . Confucius, or whomever.

As a way of thinking about what to do and who to be at any moment, this works. But it leaves little space for doubt, for the passions of living, or the consequences of risk. It reduces unhappiness by dampening expectations, and stops time by turning every present into preparation for a particular future. In this way, it creates a static society.

The problem of becoming is in being-in-time and in not despairing when the going gets tough.

Theorists of the Present

Many of us are searching for today. The modern Diogenes, no longer recognizing even the concept of honesty, is searching for the present. The world, now shrunken, pushes upon our imaginations to grasp it all at once, while paradoxically pulling upon us to enlarge it to just beyond the scope of what is handleable. This becomes a problem in our senses of time, of age, of what is long and what is short, and how do we go about finding where we are.

Where is anyone else? Is there a single now? Where I live there are two cities: one fairly much today, trying to be more so tomorrow; the other, content, a-building with some handsome version of the day before yesterday in its collective vision. Does where I live shape an outlook on today? Can it not? Does that skew my search for the present?

My sense of today as-a-teacher must include the outlooks of a shorter life, less history and more futurity, of my students: to take them through a course of study in which the present stretches out to a semester of class hours that will be remembered as a one-time thing.

Our children: Where is their today? Do we permit them their own present, or is it always some aspect of ours, which we may, or may not, like?

A large university in a small town got stuck over an

event from which it now dates itself. Ten, twelve years ago, yet yesterday in its impact on its theories of today. Will it ever change, come into today, or like some monasteries, remain in a foreverness of repose? Perhaps it should; but where do its practitioners live? How do we judge what they say about themselves and about society and . . . ? When is their students' now?

I search, I re-search each day for that day. How else to live one-day-at-a-time?

Trust Me

Listen to the intuitions, some inner voice that is truer than . . . The dreams tend to battle the observed; the observed to yield to . . . witchery.

What might happen, guesses about each next future, take over very gradually from will present will the telephone ring; what if this, why not that? This alters, then, what is observed and what is counted in the ongoingness. Attention is cast upon what might determine the next moment. The mundane and ordinary fade or are enhanced as they rejoin in new ways, in order to sharpen the vision of what has not yet been, and what is about to be. The intellect—what was the intellect—disengages and argues the shadows, boxing against sharp delineations and perpendicularity.

The dreams, the intuitions, the hopes that the dreams and intuitions are correct, overtake. The intuition, whose spaces were narrow and confined, expands beyond proportion and is given its head. What was formerly sensitive becomes mystical as the possibilities rule the whatever is.

How do we trust our intuitions, balancing them with where is here and when is now?

The Sensitive

Tuned in to the details of life, of others, I see and hear and feel what there is, and skirt also the edges of my senses. My antennae, tuned to the vibrations of activity, orifices smeared with the jellies and jams of the spaces-between, noting also what there is-not, and what there could have been. Floods of sensation, blurs of movement, the threat of overload in each moment, a threat to my integrity. What happens to my person while I respond and react to internal stimuli that I attribute to external circumstances? In order to see the world's detail, must I sacrifice my self? To what; for what?

What if I tell? Hearing more than others, seeing too much, smelling the beauty and the rot, do those others want to know what they have missed, and what they ignore? Only if they want to change? And why should anyone want to change? Whence have they come if they have not noticed how they got here?

To know what there is, to note what there is not: how to harness the roots of sensation; to redo, to accept the past that got me here; to become more without becoming less?

How can I improve vision, extend hearing, take in more, forget less ... and remain human and sane?

Journey to . . .

Castaneda's works strike me as important, in the long run: Zen turned upon itself. Instead of making the body disappear, using it as an instrument to halt time and to control itself into nothingness, Castaneda wants to make the body (every body) into a total power.

I must study every day, learning to see and to hear in the most awesomely complicated ways: extend my senses to fill all of life's experiences; not to abandon them to some promissory scheme. Life is sufficient; live it with all the care it needs and deserves.

Does it connect to rationality? Yes, in the sense that I can learn it, teach it, teach about, translate it. Much of living, especially bodily experience, remains inarticulate. The experts—musicians, dancers, artists, athletes—talk to me through their art, and do not tell me how they do what they do. To begin understanding, I must take up some bodily arts: study the cello, try to skate a straight line; become blocked, break though to some next insight; move on. Here there are models of expertise and excellence and becoming. They must be tested, tasted, chewed upon to explore life's edges and next possibilities.

To move on, to change, I must suspend disbelief as well as belief: how to think about which possibilities;

examine assumptions, presuppositions; having once discovered them, to alter them in part or in whole.

In this confusing era the time in which we readmit the human body as an important aspect of our conceptual baggage, of the fundamentals upon which being rests; the bedrock of becoming?

Extend the senses of our senses?

Work Is Life

Rather, life is Work.

Like Truth, Work is not merely what I do, but who (Who) I am.

Work is character; its development requires and demands careful thought and cultivation. It is not the drudgery of today, but the idea that the drudgery is productive of my self; that it is discipline toward the exploration of life; who I am that I could be that I would be . . . will to be.

Life is Work for life.

Success

Shapes character. But often subtly and indirectly. Success is relatively long term; incentive is in each next moment. Why should I?—to succeed! But how to conceive success in a secular world? Or in one that seems sacred?

To gain success?—money, for?—adulation?— gifts?—honor?—knowing—fame—a vision of destiny?

Success . . . destroys. What motivated was; and is no longer, if I have achieved . . . success. Working toward, is not at all having arrived. Success is a story about why I work, what I work at, what sustains that work. Success destroys, because its achievement no longer sustains, and I am empty, perpetually trying to cash in the empties and get the same refill.

But we are all already successful. Beyond what we once were, we are . . . successful. Access to whatever locked doors we now possess, and did not previously, we have achieved success. But it is no longer what it was. It was what will be, and now is what it is, merely. Thus it no longer serves to grant success, and must be reinvented, recalculated.

Success gives access to more difficult tasks. What appeared in my youth to be success, always meant less work, a deserved rest and break from routine. Instead, it has turned out to be more work, more difficult.

My Calendar

It is perhaps obvious that success in the modern world means to possess a calendar.

I have a calendar. I am a success? I gave my calendar, which fits into a pocket, to my spouse, who is becoming successful enough to need/rate a calendar. In my world, all of us are given free calendars. And I gave mine away. What can this mean?

Some of my colleagues have two calendars: one they have, one they give to a secretary or assistant. To have two calendars . . . aha! Real success. If I want to see them, I am directed to the real possessor, the one who fills in the dates. What else have the owners of the calendars given away, hidden within these sheaves of time?

Not I. I leave my calendar just where it is, on my messy desk; just so messy that I have trouble finding it. I didn't used to be cluttered; but now I am, just enough that I keep the calendar half-hidden, both to my sight and to my mind's eye. I rarely miss a date or an appointment, so it must be that I have decided to own my own calendar. Have I lost success? Have I found today?

And tomorrow?

The Serious Person

"Is that a serious question? A serious comment? Are you a serious person?" St. Augustine is reputed to have said.

"Serious," I thought. "I'm so serious that I am serious about being serious. Ready to die for my ideas, I would prefer the martyr's death and life (with not so much pain, thank you!). Serious? Questions of death and of life, of myself and others, of society, of what was and will be . . . that's what I think about. That's how serious I am."

"So?" She says: "So? We're all serious. To be oh, so-o-o-o serious, is to be in love with the idea of being . . . serious. Vanity: a new cosmetic dressing-up of old human foibles. To be serious is to like and be and do. A global thinker?—I am. For me, that is not difficult. It is not serious; it is what I am and how I do. It was not planned. It was me; it is I. Tomorrow: another day. So?"

"As for me. I am not so serious I would like to be God. To be God . . . well, that's serious. That's quality. I would love, like Augustine, to be a saint or a prophet, to be what I am and more, besides. Vanity? Be serious!"

Quid Pro Quo

Another of the great balancing acts of life: the entering into mutual debt. I owe you; you owe me. The problem is in-building, and in not-robbing the synergy of mutuality.

The temptation: to use you to construct a version of me that I find lovable. If that is/seems not possible, to use you to construct a version of me that I despise. In either case, I can yield responsibility for what I am that I like or that I hate, and yet stand outside. And so I can, with your help, stand outside of myself and become the you that has made me what I am. But am I any longer my self?

As for you: do I see you in my terms, or in yours? I can, within a reasonable version of tit for tat, give you a set of stories about you that will please you; that can devastate you. Either kind, I can find a kind of pleasure in; a justification as a someone who cares.

How to find the other-in-myself that will sustain us both? It requires mutual theories of becoming, in which promises made are updated; and the major promise is to look at today, toward each of our becoming what we can and what we would.

Being-in-Opposition

J. Bitch and moan! You're wrong; you're nasty! I'm right? Who are you? Why are you? Look! Here's how it is . . . I'm certain . . . at least I'm certain that you shouldn't be certain about . . .

H. I am! I am not! Why don't you like me? I am not likable; I like being loved. If you love me, then you must be weak, and mistaken, because I am not . . .

J. I am better than that! You must work hard to deserve my love, because I have to work so hard to be good enough to like myself. No one can like me because it's impossible to be good enough. All actual loving is fakery. But I want it; I need it. I can only settle for what there is, but . . .

The Teacher

I am/have become a teacher, I say, while more than half denying the validity of that state and of that statement. No teacher am I, I say. It's all an error, a mistake. No doubt I teach, am the teacher. But that's all a state of mind, a doingness; being-a-teacher while I teach, but then not. I am ready always to quit; my bags half-packed, seeking some sort of retreat, of safety from teaching, from myself as-teacher.

I teach from the position of what teaching (good teaching) would be like, if I were a teacher. Never actually being a teacher relieves me of certain burdens. It alters the senses in which I must feel and take responsibility, giving me a more definite, more findable position from which to think and consider what to do. Because the actual responsibility of teaching seems awesome and impossible, no real person could bear it unless teaching another's teachings. But to teach myself as subject matter is impossible unless I remove myself to some such position as I am writing from, in this moment. How to be a Real Professor?

While teaching a course is exciting and joyful, the proper view is from hindsight: to know what a course is (was). Here, the view from afterward, there are all/ none of the rewards of teaching. My life is, is bounded, and I can live my own day. The pains that enabled the joys are able to be dealt with, and I am freer to think once again. Since I can never be a good enough teacher, I can at least now balance what happened with what might have been. The view from before the course, marvel of marvels-to-be, has carried the pains and disappointments; while the present became a necessary better.

Now, with a measure of relief, I am freer to think once again. And to plan the next course . . .

Performing

As the world is theater, so life is performance. Being public, however, acting the display that is an aspect of myself, seems different; special. It requires an act of "getting-up" psychically, for some time-delimited, place-specified activity. It feels like it needs rehearsal, a sense that something will happen. There will be an audience; I may do brilliantly, decently, poorly, fail, lose heart ... And I must "come down" from the high of performance to a psychic level through which I can sustain being ... and get up another time. I crash to new lows, having performed badly or brilliantly because the cost of getting up for the performance must be paid. And many performers begin to use the high or the low to get themselves out of whatever is the opposite.

Performing is showing some aspect of character that is skilled, accomplished, special. Like beauty, performance is more than itself, an illusion. The audience sees not (merely) what there is, but also what it wants to see or to hear. Performing is to present to that audience a form of theater that the audience believes is theater is real. Performing is to suspend most aspects of self, enhancing my outsides and controlling that which is perceived. There is a tension between what the performer does and what the performance is. It is deeply tempting to become the "is" rather than the "does," on the part of each of us, as performer. And this is part of the paradox of being, in scenes where we are not exactly who we are.

But we can become; and the problem is to choose well, what we can do well, and to gradually articulate the prior illusions of ourselves-as-performers into some present reality. The trap is to become the extrinsic, the shell of the illusion, rather than what is good for self; and for others.

Hard-Times People

Most people do well in good times. They learn their trades, ply them constructively. They keep the world in its ordinary meanderings, rocking gently to and fro. They don't ask too much, are happy with the world as it acts in terms of their descriptions of it. They fend off their critics (reasonably, for good-times people own the concept of reasonableness), as malcontents; as they live upon their own surfaces.

The others, the malcontents, critics, question askers, fuss and fume and fulminate in good times. "Can't you see . . . ?" they ask. And it is the wrong question, or the wrong way to ask the question. For the G-T people see clearly and well, what they think there is to see. And it works; and who can say that it doesn't. "History—the future?— well, these are modern times. Those things don't happen anymore. There are agencies and institutions to take care. And they work well enough."

"For whom?"—scream the H-T people . . . "Can't you see what's coming?" They see the contented, the successes in that world as the ostriches; heads deeply in the sands of no-time, their asses stuck up in the air, waiting . . . to be . . .

The H-Times people: gloomily waiting for doom and hard times; so they gain an arena, a place to work; problems whose solutions are wanting, solutions whose questions have yet to be heard, even to be asked. "Listen, listen, listen!"

And some are wonderful people, the hard-timers. But bad things happen to them in good times. They get battered: hither and yon, their once clear minds focus on their own battered histories. "Vengeance!" some cry. They experience personally, what was directed toward their ideas and the styles in which they were embedded. And many become bitter, their H-T ideas now mere blurred outlines inscribing their memories or what might have been, what they would have done, if . . .

Others become exactly what they opposed. Clean thoughts, clarity of vision remains in blunt outline, the centered and central substance confused with what was outside and opposed, and the entire matter collapsed into maintaining boundaries. Meaning was blunted, gradually disappeared or was destroyed.

"On the road to hard times," became a well-defended critical nihilism, whose statement and defense became confused with positive knowledge. And it was: "in or out," or it became "out or in." It no longer mattered, and no one could tell; least of all, the critical nihilist. "For me: against me." It all reduced to the politics of charisma.

Still, a few others turn in to themselves, trying to think-out, to write a description of what happens to hard-timers in good times. Trying to be ready, waiting for a call, toughening in their mostly self-imposed loneliness.

Waiting for hard times . . .

V

The Study of Character

———•◦•———

Character is destiny.

Heraclitus

Holding Still

Steady. Study. Hang on.
Who are we? Who made us?
How did we become our selves?

The myths of objectivity,
Of knowing our selves as others know us
Become the story of our own becoming

As we write our own stories,
As they are told to us,
We are our own studies in self.

Hold still, my self
That I may see you, study you, know you,
And become the character that I would be.

The Paradox of Character

Other persons (and our selves) are simultaneously more alike and more different than we usually believe.

People everywhere in the world who deal with similar problems and issues have wide bases for common understanding, regardless of cultural history, language, personality, nationality. About farming, farmers are very much alike: concern with soil, weather, crops, the calendar, and seasons. New parents all understand one another within the vastness of what is obvious and necessary.

At the same time, people change continuously in directions that are both internal and external, and we develop each her/his own character: distinct, integrated, often cohesive. Each two persons who live together for many years—with millions of common experiences—are worlds apart on certain issues . . . And every day is new.

It is unwise and (and unsafe) to underestimate such differences or to overestimate similarities.

Also, many good, sympathetic friends can renew a conversation at a current and progressive time and space, even after not conversing for several years.

Character-as Self

Character is concerned with (describing) what a person is, and is like: how I got here; how I go about being and becoming.

Character is an interactive notion in the sense that I construct reality with respect to how others claim and believe theirs to be. At the least, it is never separable from my assessment of how others operate in their as-if worlds. I am not only judged by others, but assess their judging of me in terms that are very similar to, if not exactly shared with, my judges.

A person's existential separateness, my ultimate sense of freedom and independence, even, is constructed with the contexts and roles of others-in-mind. The notion of independence is, itself, a construct that is interactively derived; at least negotiated. It is not inherent (in any deep sense) in the individual. Character is thus a (the) notion of self; perhaps a description of the notion of self; probably both.

Character is interactive—not only socially—but also in the sense of it being some mix of active and passive. I act as if I can talk, be creative in all of the classical senses: be rational, intentional, willful. But even this demand is interactive. I am passive in the sense of being a (usually) willing recipient of others' definitions of the world. It may not even occur to me that I am receiving any more than sense-data! But I am active because others demand it, and furthermore demand that I demand it of my self. Thus it is very difficult to separate analytically, the aspects of my self that are truly active/passive: as self or as analyst. In fact, I can only infer that I am a social presence because others share a feature of being with my self, my assumption being that common features derive in some way from common sources or experience.

Character is timeful. It is stable, at least chunk-ful, because others treat us as stable and continuous. This sets up a tension between our internal readings of self, deciding who we are, knowing who we are, whence we have come, where we might be going. If we feel that we are in some senses in flux (even, say, concerning full bladders, becoming tired, refreshed), this flux is interpreted with respect to our senses of stability of self; that is, these changes are (really cyclical and recurrent) within a longer construction of my self. They are usually predictable, manageable. Some states of being are interpreted by self to be within the longer-stable pictures of self that are confirmed, perhaps provided by others. We would not know that these cyclical changes were normal if we didn't have longer self-views in terms of which we characterize our own characters!

Character is timeful, also, because we treat the external world, to a large extent, as stable. The world of objects, the ways in which we construct and sense and interpret it, is continuous in our conceptualization. We note the ordinary, but we especially note the unusual, and have ways of returning it to the usual, and of replacing our selves as observers of the world; not as experiencers in the world. We maintain our selves as if we were steady observers.

Character is not our selves in any given, fixed sense because the very definition of who we are and can become is derived from how others think about what is, and what is possible. We play within an arena that we do not create independently. Character is thus tied spiderlike within a web of extrinsic construction: not precisely of who I am, but of what it means to be someone. If I contemplate changing my character, it is within an already constructed context that is, itself, negotiable in a changing society. But, in some times and places, the size of the negotiable arena is tiny. In others, the actuality of change is largely possible and only perceptions of the possibilities are limiting: why to seek teachers or curers; at least in such times.

Character is my self in other senses, because others observe me as if I have some independence. Herein lies the tension between a person-as-self and as-others, because the observations are made within others' ways of seeing; ways that are cultural in the sense of their having general categories of thought/speech within which, and from which they observe. I am not observed in any clear, neatly bounded sense, but as I am or am not like the observers' pictures or stereotypes of someone like me.

Because we both are, and are remote from our selves as character, character can become an entity: a thing and persona to be studied and pondered; to be like; to work at; to study as if I am the actor or actress in an (my) unfolding script.

In certain times (right now?) it appears to us that there are no scripts, exactly. Thus we must invent them, give in to some extrinsic definition, go back to roots and origins, or die merely.

It is tempting—in such times—to seek for stability, thence certainty. Perhaps they appear to be the same, once we have made the move toward stability. A notion of certainty, of absolute, seems to provide a solution to the dilemmas of character: a ready-made persona; things to do, parts to act out, others to like and to dislike, rites to perform, ideas to reject and to accept as if they are my self. The world is transformed as others come to act as if I am the self that I am acting on theological or political grounds, and it furthers the movement into being that persona.

Except that it may not fit. It may rub at the big toe, press on the ankles like a set of new boots so constructed that they do not give; and I give up before I give in and yield to that character that I thought I had wanted to become.

Character: an ongoing dialogue with my self.

Problems of Scale

When there are too many, when there are more than enough, then the way we are, and the ways in which we see and know others, change dramatically, often radically. In the small, we know one another in precious detail, in personal and familial history. We keep track and are kept track of. In the large, this ceases to be possible. We cannot know all the others, and begin to treat them as types or classes or sorts. We deal with others-as-types, much as if these types are just like individuals. We classify the individuals whom we meet as typifying their own type, or as exceptions to their types. And we are not disappointed.

People, we observe, act like they're supposed to. Perhaps it is that we observe them in certain limited ways, such that what we see is principally what we have already decided to see. As long as they do not break the boundaries of our imagination of them, every interaction confirms its own type. Thus we construct our imagination of others, in the large, on the scale beyond individuation.

Problems of scale affect us. It is possible both to enhance and to diminish others when we deal with them as types or taxa. As they remain types rather than persons such as our selves they can become Godlike, or slavelike, or ... And we can, apparently easily, deal with them as our imagination of them, so long as they do not somehow break the rules by which we bound our imaginings of them. Thus the people become classed, and the classes are enduring as our memories, and beyond.

Problems of scale permit us to be kind and to use new energies, since it is possible to reduce the level of interactions to some reasonable minimum, or to the level of what we have decided, or been told in some previous time, is reasonable. Much more can get done if personal interaction becomes routinized. The cost is that life becomes technique. This, then, is carried over to our imagination of self as well as of others: the bureaucratization of the future?

In this sense of scale, persons who live in-the-large (civilized?) also become more abstract. This is not necessarily due to increased intelligence, but to the habits of dealing with the world as embodied by types. We have, in many ways, to keep track of much less, and can organize our minds by schemes that derive from talk-about, rather than from personal/interpersonal experiences.

Problems of scale may exhaust us because we interact not with others, but in our imaginations with our constructions of them. Changing times accelerate as "they" appear benevolent or fearful, decreasing our own size to the Lilliputian heroics that do not convince us of tomorrow.

The problem: how to see who we are, and who we are that they say we are, while being moved around on the scales and measures of our own times.

At a Distance

There are a number of senses in which there can be said to be a national character, some ethnic, or group character: customs, habits of thought, outlooks. The dangers in this character-izing (assuming the emergence of the taxonomist) is that these differ from group to group; from time to time. National Character implies that people who live together, or in terms of a common belief system (or both), are very likely to have some common features of being.

Surely a linguistic dialect is one of these. In the case of dialects, the differences or similarities that are apparent depend to a great extent on the nature and perspectives of the observer. A "local" will attend to personal or familial differences; a person from the next town will "hear" the dialect differences between her town's speech and what she observes; the "outsider" will not hear the distinctions, often, between full-blown languages. For example, all the Slavic languages sound somewhat "alike" to my untrained ear; or, "Romanian is the language that sounds Slavic to me, but which I can understand a good bit of, via Spanish."

The same is true of faces. Familiarity, closeness, speak of attention to certain orders of detail. At precisely what point in our seeing does a "grouping" of facial features become a social/racial "type"? To which observers?

Any of these perspectives may be valid (or invalid) with respect to the accuracy of observation, because focus tends to be very different. Locals tend to miss, or to dismiss, the very features that strike the outsider so strongly and often accurately: e.g., most Americans, regardless of background walk more similarly to one another than to anyone else, so most foreigners can identify us by our walks. Yet we insiders tend to miss this level of observation because we note the details of walking of particular ages, groups and individuals, by the ways we habitually classify them.

Without going through a number of exercises in observation, standing outside of our usual experience, it is difficult to gain insight into what may be more unusual aspects of human life. That is, many of the problems of studying character inhere in our well-ingrained, ordinary observational habits.

How, then, to stand outside our selves and our habits, in order to return with new sight about who we are and how to see? How to become a "field" worker, "a participant-observer in our own lives?

Toward an Anthropology of the Ordinary . . .

The Study of Character

How do we go about determining the structure of other persons' characters—our own? How do others think; what do they think about; what will they do in any particular situation; what do they like, dislike— why? What are the content, context, and flow of their inner dialogues? How will they sustain life in themselves?—and in their significant others ... and in us?

In the modern world and in many "primitive" worlds, the character development of any person is complicated, and continues, for most, throughout life. What facets of life turn out to be significant in any lifetime, are dependent to a large extent on features outside of inner being. Thus the study of character cannot simply be a listing or taxonomy. It must be dynamic in the sense that it must include a sense for how a given character will read, evaluate, and respond to any new moment.

The study of character must include the study of character development. It must not only be existential in the sense of my being-as-such, but it must include a "life scan," a study of how character comes to be: how I am, as a double statement about how others imagine me to be, and how I endure this external imagination; adopting parts, rejecting others, reimagining and redoing my sense of self. It must be a study of being-in-time: how else to understand being "too young" or "too old"? How do I decide the time is right or ripe? A perspective of being-as-becoming seems to characterize those who continue to grow. Some others see themselves from the universe of the fully formed.

Body image is an entry to the study of character. Here it is clear that change is inherent in being. How does my image of body-self develop, change; how is it managed? How do I accept my aging face—and yours? What does "pain" mean? How do I exorcise it, or live it? Who listens to the body; who hears it; who believes what she hears? Who changes? How do I seek (new) direction, and let go of pasts, sufficiently?

Psychologies That Underlie

A colleague once said that the behavioral sciences rest on "simple psychologies." I reacted to that in the context of his justifying a particular form of psycho-biology, by accusing him primarily of doing "politics."

Yet he is right in many senses; that each way of thinking about humans and human nature carries with or is impelled by a psychology, a way of thinking about or of depicting the individual. How a person thinks, exists, is motivated; how he judges his own worth; how she learns and when; what he values; how she conceptualizes personal life, personal living, and constructs notions of personal death; how she attends and to what; how he manages, sustains; what are her positive virtues?

The "simple" part is simply silly: the economists' notion of "greed equals rational" is short, perhaps, but not simple. Self-preservation, power, vanity, fear, approbation—none is simple. In fact, each of these can be used—is used, and has been used—to construct a behavioral science or a theo-politics. Each psychology: a discipline?

Merely because *few* practitioners of economics, or of anthropology, or of behavioral biology, do not spell these out—or are unaware of having such a theory of the individual and his psychology—doesn't mean they don't possess one. They must. Even a nonmotivational theory in a context, against a backdrop of such theories, is itself a theory; perhaps a countertheory, in an active sense.

Inattention to underlying psychologies leaves a kind of intellectual vacuum in an unnoticed place, which can be, and often is, used to spell out a view of human nature that is persuasive, especially as some unstated psychology fills a felt need in the market of ideas.

Perhaps the "ghost of time" is the magician and illusionist who occupies the spaces between our observational categories, and convinces us that we have simple psychologies.

Culture Stereotypes Character

In any societal setting a number of typical or stereo-typical characters seem to arise. As earlier studies of American or English or Russian Character suggested, there were fairly distinct types that were one or another "nationality." These studies also suggested that those qualities of national character would be seen best from the outside, from the distance of another culture. We could barely transcend our own cultural blindness, being boxed inside.

Granted there is something to the notion of a cultural or national character, we may ask how such characters develop, how the notion of character is sustained in particular settings. What is there about the experience of being or becoming a "Bongo-Ingo" which is different for being/becoming a certain sort of person? Do different cultures produce different characters, or do they somehow emerge in particular settings? Are there overlapping or characterological similarities across certain cultural functional bound-aries; i.e., do similar conditions produce the same sorts of character, at least sometimes (geography, urbanity, first child-ness)? What is the causality of character, and where can we seek to study it?

In ethnic or minority settings within a larger/ minority society, it appears to me that each such community tends to operate in terms of a limited number of stereotypes. These are active images and pictures of the characters in each world, and what they are like: a characterological map.

What this entails is an interpersonal dynamic in which the adults of a community (or their representatives: teachers, youth leaders, police) tend, fairly literally, to "see" children as if they fit into one or another of these categories. This involves, for example, responding to each child not as that individual purely in her or his own terms, but responding to a close approximation; i.e., to the child-stereotype who happens to talk or to look or to act pretty closely to the actual child. The children seem to respond in kind, by adopting or becoming the creatures of the adult stereotypes.

My personal sense (being one of those who resists, rather than adapts to the stereotypy) is that the limitation on types tends to occur only in certain settings—particularly when there is perceived to be an effective "outside" that is both defined by, and defining of, the "inside": e.g., ethnic, gendered, ageist.

The trick—for us observers—is to train our selves to remember to look not through our own personal/cultural stereotypes, but to attempt to read them in terms of the "actors" as they construct their universes: as they construct and read character.

The dilemma—for us observers—is to find some solid ground from which to observe self-consciously what others observe, merely.

Cultural/Cognitive Shifts

A friend writes about the cognitive shifts that occur in a society whose economic outlook shifts from theories of "limited" to "adequate" goods.

In the first, the entire economy is seen to be a closed box, and personal competition is the key to success. When, however, there appears the notion of adequate goods, we can work hard for ourselves, not merely against others. The very conduct of (working) life thus alters: perhaps, overnight. What we do, how we think, evaluate self and others, changes in major ways.

Anthropologists, dealing with small societies, have tended to believe that the "limited good" idea is in some deep sense "Cultural," thus not very susceptible to change. Culture—has often been used as a concept that stands for stability; or that has taken on its own force: a thing—which is considered to govern thought and imagination. From actual cases, it is apparent that the shift from an outlook of limited to adequate goods may occur virtually instantaneously; if the conditions are correct, and if perceived to be the case. The claim that rapid change could not occur because of Culture is a mistake. Change must be considered to be the underlying case, and continuity needs to be examined: to discover how it is maintained!

If we stop assigning to Culture the virtual control of how people think themselves to be, then we can begin to understand how large- (or small-) scale cognitive change may occur.

First, the dynamics of character development, in a relatively closed society, have a lot to do with the characterological map of the society, its rules and parts. What, who I am, who I can be—is determined by the members of my society. If the society is essentially closed, the numbers and sorts of character that (can) occur in that society are delimited and limited, if not always defined exactly. The closed culture operates to define persons in such ways that who I can be and who I am are finely shaped to the "demands" of the characterological map that is operating.

Why this map is continuous can be seen in the dynamics of what is considered reasonable within the ideas of the group members in any era. (Here, I extrapolate from the academic disciplines I have studied operating.) The limits or boundaries on what is "in" or permissible as part of anyone's character structure, are easily discoverable merely in the common commentary of everyday conversation wherein we discover quite quickly who we cannot be.

As this process is dynamic in essence, change can occur quite easily and rapidly as the boundaries of what a person's character is, are expanded. If my significant others are also in flux cognitively, then it is difficult for them to remember exactly who I am supposed to be, from a mapping in which they may no longer find themselves.

Declining Times

A sense of character in a time of decline . . .

Surely we are in such a phase, a time when the question of assumptions gets raised. Raised, because other stories/all our stories no longer work, or they don't make sense. A time for prophecy, a time for returns to origins, to reinventions of history, bonds; who I am, who we are together, individually.

Is what is wrong, wrong with the world or wrong with me? Why am I like I am: change, growth, making sense? Who can make sense when there are no other sensible people? But this is only the dilemma of those who don't live with others, or live only with their constructed fantasies of others. The antidote: pay attention to others' claims of who they are; they may be accurate.

The development of character in a time of decline, at least when it is first recognized and responded to, is to pull in, into my self, to discover self-ness. Rather, it is a time of me-ness, of noticing that there is something wrong. But it also makes a lot of difference whether we developed and grew up prior to such a time or within it. If we merely live it, then how are we to recognize the differences, the decline?

Is it necessary to experience a sense of progress, at least of steady-state, to notice decline? What sorts of times, of *Zeitgeists*, produced which sorts of people?

High-risk-takers develop in times of plenty, where to-morrow will be "better" than today, for example. Those who experience adversity early in life seem always to be glaring into the depths beyond good times.

The turning in to one self produces a new sort of mentality, and of mental health and illness.

Who declines in tune with declining times? Who opposes a decline? Which takes more strength? It seems much easier to intimidate, to be relatively strong in such a time because most people run scared.

Power is different in times of decline, than in good times. It is easier to gain great power—Godlike power—because, in declining times, we are susceptible. But susceptible to what? The same sort of leadership, of charisma, of style doesn't sell equally well in different times, in different sorts of times.

Does my act sell, do I sell, gain power; who has a selling style; who learns the style that sells at a particular moment?

Who endures? Who sustains?

How can we step outside of each time so that we may see what is happening and how we are affected; effecting?

How can I avoid being the logician or the anti-logic of every time, and to work at my own destiny? You? Destiny . . . ?

Reading Character

The major problems in reading character are not of traits but of dynamics. If a person is such and such, like a . . . , not a . . . , what is he going to do in a particular situation?

Can I change and become more, transcending my own history, moving past envy and vengeance to become someone I could respect, someone whom love could deserve? Will I still be a student of (my) life, when . . . ?

To read character we must keep developing and refining theories of society, of situations, of persons. To locate character, we must know what is ordinary—what is situational, what is personal—what is dynamic, and where is there stasis. To read, we must practice, and get beyond wanting the exotic to emerge; so we may see what there is, yet be open to surprise. To read, we must study our own habits of observation, watch our selves watching; become our own students . . .

And in our readings, we must study how others read, what they see and wish and think they see; how their readings affect their activity, promote or impede their own self-development. In much of modern America, for example, we tend to read and to judge character of others on the bases of "strength" and of "weakness." This judgment gains its power because we each read the character of others with respect to how we judge our selves on the same axis.

The temptation: to judge others as we hope they judge us.

The antidote: to become the person whom we can judge well ... each next day.

A Smooth Performance

A prepared talk I gave on a twenty-year-old problem was said to be very smooth. A low-paid monologist is what I said I was. For twenty years I've been waiting to deliver that speech; waiting . . . for an audience of nonstudents, of peers, of anyone who might take it seriously, or at least listen thoughtfully; or give me a difficult time, a good argument, an eloquent dismissal . . .

And there would be an audience!

I was very nervous and prepared too little, not knowing they would understand; and they seemed to. So I recouped and went on to say where it had begun to lead me—as a setting-up for a next talk to the same group. And an inner panic was reduced to a smooth delivery: "controlled, knowledgeable, interesting."

The relationship between inner states and external observables is thus often inobvious, especially among the experienced.

Character Analysis

What is (in) a character, and how do we go about knowing what someone else is . . . like?

This question is silly in a way, because all of us are already analysts of character; ours and others. In knowing anyone, we judge with respect to some judgment of self: who I am-not; as well as of who you are. Rarely do we get to see who you are-not, whom you would be, how you see who I may become. So the question of character analysis begins by re-searching our own habits of characterizing character.

Who are you . . . like? Do you like your self right now? Why? Should I like you; be like you?

Why do I ask? Do I want to know you, to use you, control you, do bad things to your person? Am I teacher, doctor, preacher, lover, lawyer, cop? Significant in your thinking about your self? Not?

Do you fit in, do you offend my ideas of what should be, do you bend my stereotypes, fit them uncritically, force me to make you an exception?

Does your presence affect how I am, how I feel? Does your presence calm me, excite me; cause me to steel my nerves, tense my lips? Does your presence force me to change in ways that I must do something to . . . ?

Do you lurk in my imagination—cropping up to fill lazy moments? Do you crowd out what I am, what

I do? Or do you disappear, an image fixed pointedly for a single moment, its edges urged to reform the backdrop?

In what situations do I know you with others, alone in the crowd or in the silences of some depth? Do I get to query you, to ask you to be analytic of your self? Will you respond to my queries? Why? Do you wonder at me? Why?

Do we see each other in the futurity of our respective becomings?

Varieties of Strength

It seems that there are several types of personal strength, all of which might appear to be similar: strength from constituency; strength from upbringing; strength from adversity/survival; strength from success; and so on.

In selecting juries, for example, the sorts of strengths or weaknesses of potential jurors may be terribly important in their being partial, or being able to suspend belief. Those who appear strong because they have had earlier success, may be currently vulnerable; likewise for those whose strength is obtained from the support of others ... if those others no longer exist, is strength really there?

The strong-appearing people, therefore, may or may not be actually strong at any moment. We may be dealing with external style whose depth is less than shallow. And the relationship between strength and integrity is crucial in the study of character. Integrity is in becoming stronger, but especially in estimating our own strength honestly.

People estimate others, often then testing these estimations and then re-estimate how strong they imagine others to be. We can, for example, threaten someone; if she backs down, we have a good deal of information about that person—depending on how we use, and are experienced in interpreting, a particular sort of threat.

Or a person can throw out some bait, an opportunity, a small bribe, and see how others manage it. If they take a small bribe, then I will estimate them lower and weaker than otherwise.

There is a balance point not just between strength and weakness, but also (or, rather) between strength and reasonableness. Those who deal with power, solely, operate from the vision that others also operate solely within a power matrix. The truly strong judge strength or weakness immediately, then concentrate on how rigid, open, or reasonable, others are. The strong estimate others, in the long run, on the basis of these features, more than in terms of weak and strong.

This is one of the reasons why people tend to misread one another . . . And themselves.

A Sense of History

I know that we can create an ideology for many people by restating their history. For those of us whose present and future are kept and held in balance by a retelling of past events, a rereading of certain informing texts, the ways in which we read and interpret and what fills those tellings, affects present understanding. In searching for who we are, we go back to "origins." But where they are exactly, and how they are to be read, and who says how to do this, powerfully defines today and informs how we will think about tomorrow.

Who inspires us, what frightens us, whether we blame—ourselves, our shapers, some others—is a story about time and our belief about the causes of today.

How are we told what we are like and what ties us together, is also a certain sense of history. A people, a nation, a religion, a culture? What are we; who are we-not; where are the boundaries and what is their form? Why do such stories work? When do they not?

How did we get here? What do we remember: to remember; to forget? Even the same stories change in their detail, their power to inform today. Each day: an interpretation? Each performance of the same ritual, a way to keep the world in its way?—to say who and where we are?

But times are different, and stories sell differently

in the cognitive/intellectual/vanity/fear times. Is this a time for history; for reinvention?

How do we re-create our selves, every yesterday, each today, for the next tomorrow? How can we gain ownership over the writings and readings of our own histories?

Character Shaping

Who I am, writ large.

What shapes this? Assumptions of, and about us; observations, but interpreted within some circumscribed frameworks, some finitely extensible limits. When people observe others, they see a mix of what is, and what they think they see. The nature of what is, may or may not be linked with the image.

There are some deep questions about a residual notion of ontology: "I am what's left over after the image disappears from me." Not sufficient, for I am constantly remaking my self to fit an image of self that may also be changing. Others redo me, but in different ways, usually, from those in which I reinvent my self. There are creation and reinvention "rules" that are also susceptible of being defined as we experience the world with others. If the idea of history were simple, wouldn't we realize we are aspects of it?

The tangible observation is that we (can) find places of low turbulence from which to view the processes of history. How do we find where we are in the fluxes of being? How do we locate our observational selves?

The existentialists' idea of existence as enhancing personal freedom is nowhere as clear as anyone claims. Such ideas derive from Rousseau's notion of society of community as coming in to deny or limit freedom on an individual who is born free. But we are not born free. The freedom of experience is emergent. It develops as those with whom we interact (parents, friends, teachers) help us to develop a self; a self that talks as if it has/is a will, can think, talk. Our notion of personal freedom is already shaped to some large extent, by the time we arrive at personhood. The tension between self and others seems more actually to be a tension between an actively developing idea and experience of self, and how others treat us—as if we are.

But the outside—others/society/community—is not one thing or singular in any actual fashion. To say so, is to make up a great "they" and act in terms of our personal definitions of it; never to see what "they" are or what "they" see in us, to which we live reactively.

Each new day, a study in who they are and what they see, in the character that I will to become . . .

Next Places

...on changing, developing my character. Becoming...

It is no less difficult for us to change our own characterizations of self, than for others to change their views of us. Certainly each society has positions or roles that affect the way in which any person is conceptualized. But, in modern times, which tend toward bureaucratization, the spread tends to narrow; at least appears to be narrow, especially as adolescent credentials qualify us forever in a world that toys with notions of permanent tenure. How to locate where we are?

The amount of actual time we spend with others affects the possibilities of change in wondrous ways: the more time together, the greater the paradoxical tendency both to change and to stability. If people see each other as slightly different in each moment, then acting in terms of those differences may either enhance or restrict the changes noted. The differences reside in observation, but also in anyone's fantasies of the other(s), as to their real enduring character; as well as our friends' own sense of self as highly or less dynamic.

Any friendship or group relationship can float out of sight of the reality of the rest of society. If friends respond in terms of a quick dynamic—each mood change reacted to—there is "drift." The changes, viewed from outside the relationship, often appear inexplicable. And it is difficult for the inside to gain insight into its own shifts since they had, at each moment, seemed correct and reasonable with respect to what each person saw and responded to. In effect, it is this dynamic that gives rise to family, group, ethnic, and national character: who I am, who I am like, different from, and in which ways. And, if the drift is too great, then I am (we are) perceived to be deviant or mad.

This accounts, not only for the sort of interpersonal persons a group tends to develop and to evolve, but also for the sorts of logics that emerge no less from groups than from persons (and from the perceptions of young people about groups they find attractive; e.g., religious, business, community . . .). It is important what a group does, but it is no less important how we think about it and about one another . . . Just as likely and reasonable ways to account for war and other human propensities, as the assumptions of the personal-individual battle against (social) restrictions on one's presumed birthright of freedom.

Returning to the development of our own character, now in the context of surviving the groupthink: Survival appears easy if a group's image of a person works for us, and continues to work. To work means that we can live, not too unhappily, in continuing terms of our own image and sense of self. However we do this, there is either not too much opposition to our characters and self-images, or there is some positive support for our notions of who we are. We seem to work harder and more self-consciously on our own development in terms we have constructed personally. External positive support tends to confirm us at too many, often too early points in our development, and we tend to fixate on the character that sells to a particular audience (dynamics and quality of anyone's audiences . . .) rather than working on becoming that character which we can enjoy being, can sustain and find sustaining. Occasionally we make decisions that worked out at that moment, but which have become problems in the long run. And we must get past them without discounting our own memories.

And in personal terms? Where is my next place? Do I want to be me, to be moral, to be loved and loving? Yes, of course.

Where does my search take me? Into my past—how I got here, within others' pictures of me—who they said and think I am and wish(ed) me to become; into my pictures of what can no longer be and what is just possible; of what I want and imagine that I can enjoy being; of a character who remains alive and represents a best-case outcome of a hard-lived life.

The next place?—on the road to my own way; more than yesterday with room for tomorrow. Each of us, already much defined, having to grapple with our own histories and sense for any future; ready for death and disaster, but taking life as opportunity.

Perfect? Not I. Not you. Not possible . . . within time. The test and challenge of character, of becoming, are to acknowledge death, yet live in life's terms. What perfection there might be, is my and your construction of what is perfect. The next place is to become more like your notion of what might be, neither sacrificing nor diminishing.

Fear, weakness? Me? You? Yes, and why not? That is who I am . . . and you are.

I am a teacher. I work toward your future, within my own presents. My struggle is to understand and to tell: my queries, my understandings, whence they derive and where they seem to point.

And you? Where is your next place?

Commentaries

The technological world has transformed being so that many of us can live "the longest life." As Cicero, in ancient Rome, asked, however: Given that we all aspire to live long, what are we going to do in old age? How do we construct our lives—is it even possible to "construct" a life—so that we have, as Kierkegaard expresses it, "character tasks"?

We cannot all become any particular thing, martyrs to the same cause, heroine to our own childhood imaginations. Often, life seems to move on of its own momentum, its own pace, carrying us along with it. Does it mean something to ask: Can we enter (reenter) our own lives? How? "Start the world again, and I will climb on!?"

Kierkegaard didn't know how either, but he suggested a powerful contrast for our contemplation. From the cultural "backwater" of Copenhagen in the nineteenth century, where everyone (as in the Twin Cities of Minneapolis and St. Paul) seems to "be" a Lutheran, he deplored the joining of any church and implored each of us to reenter the life of the deity: for the Christian, Christ. But, he argued, it is insufficient to join the church, to worship or become a disciple of Christ, a mere believer—this is to stand outside of our own Being, of ourselves. Instead, we should live just like Christ lived: as a close approximation, as close as humanly possible, to living as Christ . . . or Muhammad, or the Buddha, or the Great Spirit, or Jehovah, or . . . In twentieth-century parlance, we should model our lives like his, but ever more strongly and completely. Not passively to accept, but to act and live . . . thoughtfully.

Experientially, this is not so simple. Kierkegaard was steeped within a family and the church, and he reacted violently upon his twenty-fifth birthday to not having "done" anything. Most of us are raised by others, within the contexts of their life arrangements and outlooks, and we generally operate within their thinking and their outlooks. Most of us, if we enter into life crises, think rather that we have been incorrect, misunderstood, or have otherwise "messed up." It does not occur to us, in any "long-life" sense, that we should construct our character tasks. Rather, we prepare to be adults, gathering some sense of what that might mean from those we see, from family, friends, teachers, neighbors. If we experience crises of being, of insistent cries of our own being, of our existence, telling us that all is not so good, they mostly arise somewhat later in life, after we climb the rungs of our own life-ladders and are either stuck, or find that some supporting rungs have become worm-eaten.

Well, what inspired this book of meditations was the outcome of a "religious" event: the mass suicide in about 1979 at Jonestown, in Guyana. This was a most dramatic event, coming as it did within a time when many, many people seemed to be worried and were searching for . . . for something. Too, it was the reaching of our own middle age, when our children were about to jump from the nest and life seemed to in-

sist on constant evaluations . . . which were not at all
"A+."

Was it us, or the times, or the world, the
economy . . . ? It was a time to wonder what had happened, what had gone wrong, and could it be righted?
What next? How to think about it? How to regain, to
regather the strength and thoughtfulness and humor
about being, which, we told ourselves, we had loved in
ourselves and in one another.

The Commentaries offer reflections on the beginning aphorisms of *Next Places*. They attempt to
re-place or relocate each piece in somewhat different
contexts from the original. For some, they place the
poetic musing on the self into the history of thought,
particularly philosophical arguments that continue
to influence our thinking. Others consider our individual histories, and how they may shape or confine
our present being.

Next Places, rather than repeating others' ideas,
attempts to ask each of us to situate ourselves in the
present. History has to be considered, but it is not
necessarily definitional of our being today toward our
Next Places. In these senses, the Commentaries are
interpretive of the texts. They offer contexts, ways of
considering who we are, positive possibilities and sen-
sibility of where we might think and intend to go next
in our lives.

As prose, the Commentaries are also intended to
be provocative and in dialectic with the prose poetry
of the aphorisms. Rather than being definitive of any
particular understanding, they are intended more to

be paths for rethinking. Hopefully, they will inspire readers to offer their own reflections on who they are, and where they will go . . . next.

⌐· I. My Self and Myself

Each today, we awaken, get up. Whether bright or overcast, the light is not always enlightening. We carry into each moment of each day a set of tasks, of ideas, of records and tapes from various pasts that live within us, and as us.

There is a question, a wondering, a need to make problematic the present day in which I try to engage myself, versus the stuff that comes along with the package that is me. In any relationship it seems even more complicated, because the senses of self and of each other are more than doubled: me, and you, and the relationship—kids and houses and pets and food, and the losses and gains of age. Today is just tacked on to the calendar that our minds sift through.

To make problematic is to cause us to locate this moment (today), and to engage in dialogue between what was and what is: thus, the concept of "my self" and "myself." "Myself" is the lifelong calendar, the years rolled up into a carpet that hushes problems and conceals the present moment. How powerful was the frozen terror that still haunts our being today? How powerful was the so subtle self-restraining that lurks just below consciousness, blurring the edges of our being?

Just what is located in that history? How did it

shape present being? How can it be wondered about without applying the same habits to our character that enabled its earlier formulations in my character? If it was hardened by terror or by infinite practice, does it need Nietzsche's tumultuous hammer to re-form it? If it remains as the reflection of narcissistic pleasure, will it be replaced by an ugliness that is equally narcissistic in its anti-pleasure?

The pains of bodies bloated with the beers and foods and outlooks of indulgence, drugged and wanting euphorias, only to be dipped into the lowering and lowering of the after-euphorias, brought about this wonderment. Finally! Days of reckoning. It would be easier, we thought, if there had been precisely discernible crises. But part of the modern condition is that we have been fairly successful in postponement, in bargaining with futurity—literally, in insuring our lives. Nothing goes wrong, exactly! It is more a slow, oh so slow, acceding to being what we are; and requires, it seems, an oh so slow awakening.

Its texts are the texts of lights and enlightenment, beginning with Plato's *Republic* (V), read as if Kierkegaard's spirit was editing it. We have lived long within the cave, seeing the shadows dancing upon the walls opposite, lit by the unsteady undulation of poorly drafted fires, not knowing what is real (today and my self), from what is shadow (memory and myself). In first sensing the light above, outside, we rise to the surface, become dazzled by the sun's intensity and fall back, down. But the light (of today's reason), once discerned, becomes compelling. The direction is upward, onward, with a longing for (in)sight into today, so tomorrow, each next place, becomes discernible, constructable, possible.

If it was terror that shaped me, it is now an aspect of me. It must be meditated upon; not denied, not rejected. Wonder!

⌣· *The Essential Character*

The problem of identity, of being, of self is immense both within everyone's life and within the history of philosophy in many world traditions.

It arose most directly in our lives when my (only) sister said that our mother was splintered in her personality, like the character of the book *Sybil*, which was published in the early 1970s. To us, that didn't seem like a very good analysis of my mother's character, which was indeed complicated, having become somewhat "fixed" in adolescence when her family lost all of its (fair amount of) money and her own mother died of influenza. Perhaps it was my sister's projection. Perhaps . . . ?

But it raised poignantly the question of continuity and change of one's self, or being, or identity. We noted, in that era, as well, that our two children quickly and seemingly firmly understood who they were, *that* they were. And that the vast differences and changes that are apparent in anyone's photos over time are easily arranged into a history: one's history; my history. But how fragile is this sense of one self? Where does one "find" this self, and hold it together? Is it outside of

Being, a place of objectivity from which one views the world in a consistent and pure and honest way?

Philosophically, this is precisely Hume's problem of the eighteenth century, when he raised in his *Enquiry concerning Human Understanding* the skeptical question about the very possibility of objectivity, of making (scientific) observations, of being or having a self that one could "find." Who—my sister's wonderment—was "at home"? Which doors do we approach, which bells do we ring to gain entrance to the self that stands outside of the vagaries of life?

While this has never been solved exactly, philosophically, the practical aspects of technology have become effective proofs of themselves, and much of the skepticism has been swept under pragmatic rugs. It became, however, a central problem of living in the twentieth century, in which Heidegger and his myriad descendants, pondered Being, and time, and how knowledge was even possible: we are presently skeptical even about the possibility of knowing and of meaning, "driven," I think, by the sense that Being is always about to float away from our sense of self. More worrisome, skepticism about knowing easily slides into the various forms of nihilism that want to deny change and tempt us back to the texts of classical or biblical times.

Admitting its being problematic, we think it requires some doing, some existential involvement in one's being: a re-creation and reinvention, a restating of who one is, by an active consideration of personal history. In this era, personal photographs—metaphorical as they may be—are "useful" to substantiate Being.

Besides photos, we may now realize, there is only memory, and the testimony of others to certify Being. But, as the photographic survey tells us, it is not difficult to reconstruct our Being. The problem is, more, how to do it well.

⌐ On Losing Time

Life, marriage, the house, the neighborhood, the seasons, the world, wars, television . . . everything. It all became ordinary. Year upon year rolled up. The only way we were assured of the passage of time was the children's growing up. After twelve years (we thought) of marriage, after about twelve years we could no longer remember just why we married one another. It seemed OK. But everything seemed OK. Life had gone from memory to having become memorized.

It was all known: life, marriage, the house, the neighborhood, the seasons, the world, wars . . . Today (this day, some years later now), it seems all quite different, new, the memorized world deconstructed (as they say) in various ways. But then, we had become like bureaucrats, moving piles of papers from the "in" box to the desk's surface, stamping each in its boring turn; thence to the "out" box; and begin again. Kafka was becoming like life, or vice versa. It was difficult to distinguish. By this time, we knew most of the details of the plots of the novels that had earlier served to educate and to entertain. Now it was all theme and variation: and we knew all the themes, which ran about in our mind's eyes, like thematic music that had become a cliché. What wasn't a cliché?

One day, for now obscure reasons, our heads began to roll in some no-saying unison, that this was not sufficient. Perhaps it was the Schlitz beer ad that banged at being: "You only go around once."

Opposed to the poetry and outlook of starvation and oppression, for us life had become easy, too light. We longed for something "heavier," not yet knowing what that could mean.

OK.

⌣· Vision Quests

Living, doing fieldwork in the hills of Mexico, having spent a summer among the Taos Pueblo Indians in New Mexico, we had become saturated in American Indian lore. At various times, neighbors and a few friends were indigenous people. Those we knew well were strong and proud; more like the Indians of movie lore than the underclass that wanders often in our urban setting. They were thinkers, philosophers, who approached life more completely, more seriously perhaps, than others we had known. Most astonishing to us was the greater elaboration and fullness of their memories, characteristic apparently of people who do not rely on literacy and remembering only the books and newspapers of life, to locate information and invest themselves with knowledge.

In much of Americana, there is a sense that one's

being is not complete within oneself, but that being is in some ways multiple. Being is, perhaps, shared with others, particularly with the "spirits" of other species. Our spirits, or Nahuals (as they say in Mexico), are also those of some other animal, whose characteristics we take on. And we must enter, around adulthood, into some quest, to see, to seek which spirit we are. It is not so obvious; rather, it is arduous. And it must be done well, lest one offend . . . destiny, the universe!?

In the Western traditions, especially the stress on individuality and freedom and self-determination that we all enjoy (mostly), it is not so clear how we pursue our means to support ourselves. We are, we tell ourselves, largely self-determining. We "make it," we are successful within the socioeconomic world that is conceptually separate from our personal being. Yet, choices must often be made; choices often are made. And they strongly affect our futures. Which choices did I make (my father wanted to go to medical school—and I was to act this out?)?

How, today, do old quests affect Being? If they were truly vocational, serious as vision quests, they ought, as Kierkegaard tells us, be sufficiently grand for the longest life. If they were not serious? If they were developed from some adolescent fixation? Did it grow with us? Did it, did I remain a superannuated six-year-old, looking to be a space-jockey? A teenager hoping for martyrdom . . . but without too much pain?

We had, at some time, vowed to become anthropologists to our own lives. Having been abroad for three years, having seen in Mexico and in England a great deal that was interesting, and odd, and highly contrastive with the United States, we became enamored with the "ordinary." We thought, we told ourselves, we could remain distanced, "visitors" to our own lives, and live just like others . . . live, lived.

But, for us, it wasn't working very well. It was many degrees more difficult to pull off than to celebrate in imagination. It became isolated: from neighbors, from any academics who thought increasingly that anthropology meant exotic, which meant far away. And we, self-thrilled at first, had discovered how to make the ordinary seem exotic. The "so?" of J.'s positivism gradually became the "so what?" of past decisions that demanded greater strength, in the present. Or we had calculated poorly, hoping for any rescue, gradually exteriorizing hope, forgetting how to look within.

⌣· *Being as Being-Not*

Categories, taxonomies, labeling: reifying, fetishizing: including, excluding, defining: defining-in, defining-out. From Aristotle's "Categories," to the details of Linnaeus's descriptions, the wonder and puzzle of what is because we define it that way, seem at war with some notion of reality and the world in itself. Is the world? Do we know it directly through our intuitions, as our intuitions? Can we know it at all? Every century or so, reality becomes problematized, and skepticism nags at our being. Whew!

Complicated enough for the external world, how do we construct our own characters? At various moments in life, this question seems particularly alive. For us, many years were passing by; sliding by, it seems. In that same old house, same old neighborhood, we had no doubt been doing and being. Nothing terribly bad had happened; nothing much good, nothing much exciting; just "hanging in," trying to maintain, sustain . . .

All of a sudden (?) I, we, awoke to discover that our senses of self had become blurred, not exactly anywhere to be found? Where was I? Where were we? We began ... . ners, as slaves to a decrepit house, slave to some sense of the past that now seemed problematic, we began to wonder how the sense of self, of myself, and of my self had happened. Gradually then, now condensed in memory, our parents had died one by one, and we were left with memory, but without testimony.

It did not seem awful, or terrible; mostly puzzling. We seemed to ourselves, to one another, to be much the result of the reflections of others, of relationships, of once positive aspects of, say, owning a home, which had only gradually become more burden than joy.

As day dawned, like Nietzsche's "Zarathustra" retiring to his mountained seclusion, it seemed necessary to begin withdrawing, in order to see. And what we saw included the sharpness of the reflections and of the reactions. But there was little of thoughtful construction. Where were we now that we needed our selves, wanted ourselves? First, it seemed, we needed to discover, to rediscover who we are-not, which has so powerfully glossed over the passing of time. Had we mistaken the strength of reflection and not-being for something strong in and of itself?

⌣· *Living like God*

Like the story of Dr. Faustus, who sold his soul (self?) to the devil for a guarantee of possessing all of knowledge, we are tempted by the devils and poltergeists, the very beautiful and the mostly ugly. We are only human, we tell ourselves, and are told, at once with the wispy trails of other tales telling us that we are more than human. Transcendent!

It seems easier, often, to go beyond being ourselves, to some sense of what is more. But we do this with little care: care-less-ly. Just as we have "given away" experience to writers, to journalists, to movies, to radio, to marketeers, to tele-visionists, we often prefer the illusion of the stage and the desire for what we wish, to overcome Being.

I, we, have no doubt that Being is more than itself. The danger, the trap, the diminution of the self that is important and necessary to future being, is in wishing more than being; or, in wishing rather than being. Oz beckons, kismet radiates, Fate gladdens our hearts. Yet, where are we, and where am I?

At "those times," like "those days" of women whose nature exteriorizes itself, into whom nature intrudes itself, we are moreover tempted to retell ourselves ever more strongly the mystical story, the dream whose translation into life was earlier enabling.

Does it still serve? Does it still "work" in our lives, providing whatever direction or solace it did . . . once? Do we need to repeat it, more often, more shrilly? Have we lost hearing? Has the story changed, somehow, without our noticing? Do we now look for transformation, for a euphoria that intellectual and real drugs seem to provide?

Do we believe, still? Or is it now receding into the mostly hidden memories where other childhood stories reside? Is it a question of believing in our selves being and becoming more than yesterday, more than today? Is it a question of believing, still, our own old stories?

It is often very difficult to go beyond, to go over, to transcend one's past and past stories to oneself. Nietzsche posited the "Overman" (not, as he is translated into fascist thought, as "super-man"). This over-person is an aspect of one's self, which tries to go beyond each yesterday; to face the fact that today is here, likely more difficult than yesterday, needing to muster strength and enliven frailties. If we can find some notion of a deity within our characters, of the devil, or of beauty, and the mystical, surely we can find . . . our self.

Is the direction of life to be upward or downward; overcoming or yielding? Once again, from the top: do we continue to believe what we tell our selves we believe?

For us, personally, habit had become overwhelming, and we needed to move on. More, these days, I think we had become bureaucrats to our own lives. Success had turned into continuity. Change?

⌣· *The Necessary Self*

This seems more a muse than a meditation. It is bittersweet, wondering, puzzling. My sense of self, the stoic heir to the Roman sense of self-reliance—of Epictetus, especially—is so, so solid on certain days. Emerson had nothing on me. Rock hard, grounded to the very center of the earth; more, to the universe! Yet...

Yet... what? Inside, I have the cream-puff moments when I cannot muster the nerve to do what I would; what I . . . should. Why this vast range? Where does each reside? How can I find these parts, their foundations, their steadinesses? How can I augment?

What? What if it all crumbles or all turns into rock?

It seems that there is some part of my character that is really, truly necessary; which needs to be grounded in ways that I can find it, and either call a halt to the extremes, or to learn to . . . to enjoy them. Some days I seem stranger to myself, or estranged from myself.

Can I change what is necessary to change, without sacrificing what is necessary to my being?

⌣· *Being and Moving On*

We inherit from Aristotle the sense that our character is composed of certain "virtues" that are not very bound into history: they are "characterological" or "temperamental." Particularly, they are timeless; that is, outside of time. Keeping our eyes on some notion of a transcendental—on a deity, or on this timeless vision of ourselves—seems to be a useful, working self-concept much of the time. On other days, at certain interruptive (of this timeless self) moments, we may discover or become suddenly aware that the present moment does not relate particularly well to our own sense of our own history. In modern parlance, we become alone; terrifyingly alone.

I laving entered (ourselves) into history since Hegel; having entered into our own existence, finding in these odd moments that there is no longer any observational resting place, we could, following Kierkegaard, attempt to mold and to model ourselves upon the living aspects of a Christ: to attempt, not to be like Christ, but to live like Christ lived. Or we can, like Camus or Sartre, find ourselves dreadfully alone, anew each day; living, as it were, in the infinitesimal, literally shrinking.

How puzzling, how unsettling, to have uncovered a present moment that has lost its linkage with the past.

But I have merely to look at my hand to feel the literal weight of my body moving, to recall memory. Who was I, who I am, no longer? But that is not correct. Or, if it is: who am I now, who I was not before? A puzzle, or a paradox? What differs in their definitions?

The paradox is that I both change and do not; the puzzle, that I only now discover that life is sometimes paradoxical. It is Kafka and Borges whom we can study, who came upon this, this insight, and played it over and over in myriad forms.

The path toward solution is to ponder on how (I)

had attempted to "resolve" a paradox, and did it successfully, for a while. And now I discover its presence in mine, as if I am victim to my own prior adjustments. The puzzle: if I win, I lose . . .

⌣· *History versus My Next Places*

From Aristotle in ancient times, and Hobbes in the beginning of the modern, there has been a duality between the personal/psychological and the social/political: person and citizen. Now these categories are further complicated, their boundaries made fuzzy and barely discernible by their being placed within time and one's own history.

All those "wh-" questions—who? where? what? which? why?—keep arising anew in my thinking, striving to find who I am, today, not all these others, not a social entity predetermined in some Marxian sense by all the roles assigned me: a terminal case of fuzzy boundaries. It seems all more complicated than I had thought, than "they" had told me, or I had heard.

A (usually) friend has discovered a support group of Adult Children of Alcoholics, trying near age fifty to account for what his alcoholic father "did to him" during his childhood. For a long time now, he has been "blaming" his father, holding his own history ransom to the present moment; trying to redo his history by recapturing it for himself. As if, perhaps, it will help the present and enable a . . . better (?) future. There is a fine line between blaming one's past and studying it; of becoming someone else's definition of oneself, and one's own definition. The temptation toward the past, toward lolling within the categories we now think have distressed us, is that we are proprietors of our own histories.

Similarly, we can stand outside of ourselves, or outside of any notion of responsibility and of conscience, if we "choose" to dwell upon our being within the categorical sense of myself that keeps us somewhat "hidden." The fact is: I am all of these! Which? When? Which will enable and be useful, in a future in which any sense of ownership is diffuse, risky, not certain?

⌣· Perspectival Character

The question of integrity and wholeness of character, of being complete seems like another paradox of living. Yes, I am a wholeness; yes, I am many—and both seem to be true. Which and when seem to be more a matter of context and of perspective. To attempt to solve or to re-solve this apparent opposition within us in the name of some transcendent wish to stand outside of ourselves (e.g., of our bodies) may be limiting or destructive. The irony here is that the problem concerns the self, and to consider self-destruction by attempting to find some coherence and integrity in that self, makes no sense: either way, some part of "me" is lost.

Philosophically this reflects a Hobbesian criticism of the Aristotelianism in which he was educated and to which he reacted: viz., that our "virtues" are somehow ingrained within the individual, and most of living consists of their expression in various circumstances. Hobbes, who was much more inclined toward the dynamics of their expression, thought that the virtues were frequently at odds, even at war, within each person. Within the (entire) tradition of Western thought, however, there has been little question that the locus of the self is "contained" within the individual (usually in some sense of mind versus body).

I, thinking "rhetorically," consider that the concept of our being as individuals primarily has set us on wrong paths of thinking about the self. Our individuality is largely "derived" and "emergent" from interactions with others. This leads to the living paradox: that we are, at once, integral and not. Given this conceptual path, what is enormously interesting is that we do not splinter; at least, not frequently. But, the rhetorical approach permits us to see that the paradox is not to be resolved, on one side or another, but to be an aspect of our living: how to do it . . . well?

One problem is how to stay outside a war with or within oneself. Another is how to remain fairly clear that we are complicated creatures, and to remain a student of ourselves, and of how we observe the world.

One metaphor is that we possess as many perspectives upon the world as those persons who are significant counters in our memorable existence: parents, siblings, friends, mentors, deity(ies), and so on. For, it seems, we have the means to see out as each of them . . . would see.

Or, it may be, that each "age" of our own being has its own perspectives on today: ages five, eight, thirteen, twenty-one, and so on. Someone may remain a favorite, or a total reject. But they may remain, actively seeking a voice in living, a perspective upon what is now.

It is useful, possibly crucial, to remain students of our own perspectival habits. Possibly we need to understand them, to alter them, to reincorporate them into a coherence or clarity directed toward a next place in our lives.

⌣· *The Handicapped Character*

The existential problem, which is, I think, very general, is that I am not exactly who I appear to be. In my personal case, this is perhaps so clear and obvious to me that it needs no commentary. On the other hand, it is a sort of lie, a "passing" and an attempt to be someone I am not, really. Modern surgery and modern cosmetology allow us (encourage us) to alter our appearance; to be someone . . . else? Do I lie to others? To myself? What is wrong with appearing natural; ordinary?

Several metaphors have guided my thinking: in a human anatomy course, all the students were assigned to research an anomaly of the cadaver they were dissecting. Everyone, it seems, is anomalous in some sense or other; aware or not. Ordinariness, not to mention perfection, is some rhetorical or semiotic construction that we impute to others or to ourselves: self-images, which are often very powerful in various senses of what we may mean by "integrity."

Another metaphor was derived from a Mexican movie, in which a youth lost one eye, in a culture in which damage or imperfection is not regarded lightly. On the other hand, there is an active "beggar" culture there, a place for the infirm, the less than ... The obvious resolution to the youth's problem was to blind himself. This he did, finding a living solution to a problem of imperfection.

In America, a cartoon in the *New York Times* suggested, the majority of the population is truly blind: here, the one-eyed man is king!

In the history of ideas and philosophy, not much is made of handicaps, while much is made of personal beauty. For the ordinary amongst us (and the ordinary within each of us) there is little guidance, except perhaps to "forget ourselves" and to praise the beauty of others. One feels strongly a utopic wish here, a paean to life, and a sense that imperfection is tantamount to a tasting of death. Perhaps the story of Snow White, wherein the beauty of youth fairly directly "causes" the aging ugliness of the middle-aging, resonates within our calculations. Alas! Lost youth, beauty.

Alas, the sobbing over loss, the difference from the regular, the lessening of my appearance (living in the knowledge that the appearance belies every reality), doesn't do much to inform today, or add much energy to the towardness of futurity. The living problem is how to accept our realization of what is, and not to lessen our being because of it. How to live with, and to move beyond ourselves, without invoking the transcendent, eternal, or utopic that serves to deny rather than to inform?

One of my teachers (Ray Birdwhistell) once said

that there are two types of people: cripples and crippled cripples. In various senses, in different moments, all of us are crippled. How do we avoid being cripples whose gimpiness calls sadness to its own attention?

⌣· The Foreseeable Future

Sophistication seems to be at war with Pollyanna and the Bluebird of Happiness. The bulk of the philosophical literature (in Western thought, at least) seems to presume that the world is pretty "steady" in its orbits and trajectories. Even when time is inscribed within the orbitings, when the phenomenology of existence places us within our own being (Hegel), it remains tempting to construct the foreseeable future in our personal terms of what is history. Even when history is destiny, we find ways to stand apart. Always, it seems, we are tempted to stand outside ourselves, in some pose-transcendent: visitors to our own lives. Searching for the "salvation" of our souls, we disattend . . . to our bodily being and presence.

We fall into strange (bad?) habits. Addiction, I believe, is to imagine the foreseeable future, inevitably and inexorably, with us and our "habit" linked: no matter how far forward we can "project" it.

But there are also philosophical-theological attempts to "destroy" history, which illuminate the question of optimism and its opposite category. Messianic Christianity, in its premillennial form, predicts that the Messiah will rejoin us (again) after

1,000 years—around A.D. 2000. In that moment, it will be as if the millennium had not occurred—our "souls" exist timelessly, eternally in whatever paradise we may imagine. Zen Buddhism attempts to concentrate and to focus all our being in each moment, to background, even deny history and our earthly existence—except as . . .

The issue of optimism has much to do with the concept of the foreseeable future because of its notion that "things" will get "better" or "worser." How long is this future? How will it get filled? How do the answers to these queries get answered in any next moment? How are plans, toward the future, constructed? How do they get actualized?

Silly or weak optimism (rescue me, oh prince-cess!) is wont to presume that tomorrow will be better: so why not wait to do anything? A similar, weak pessimism expects nothing, so nothing happens, each day.

A stronger optimism may attempt to construct the foreseeable future "generationally," to my grandchildren. It always, though, in its intellectual phase, sees the worst possible outcomes; accepts, as the definition of philosopher in Plato's dialogue "Phaedo," one's own demise, and looks back at life thusly, gaining strength. But the possibility of losing resolve, the problematic of sustaining and stretching the foreseeable future, is always "at risk." How to maintain and fortify this vision so that it enables each day, each day?

Pessimism, which has a strongly intellectual phase, tends to foreshorten the concept of the foreseeable future, often looking back to history or to a "golden age." In this way, "today" can be affirmed as a reenactment, and its business conducted . . . as always.

How can I discern these tendencies within myself? How can I construct the future, well—and find some balance between a mortal desire always to lengthen it, and the human acceptance of this being "just another day"? And what of the question of change and the "new"?

To order additional copies of *Next Places*

Web: www.itascabooks.com

Phone: 1-800-901-3480

Fax: Copy and fill out the form below with credit card information. Fax to 763-398-0198.

Mail: Copy and fill out the form below. Mail with check or credit card information to:

       Syren Book Company
       5120 Cedar Lake Road
       Minneapolis, MN 55416

Order Form

Copies	Title / Author	Price	Totals
	Next Places / **Harvey Sarles**	$14.95	$
		Subtotal	$
		7% sales tax (MN only)	$
		Shipping and handling, first copy	$ 4.00
		Shipping and handling, ___ add'l copies @$1.00 ea.	$
		TOTAL TO REMIT	$

Payment Information:

__ Check Enclosed __ Visa/MasterCard		
Card number:	Expiration date:	
Name on card:		
Billing address:		
City:	State:	Zip:
Signature:	Date:	

Shipping Information:

__ Same as billing address __ Other (enter below)		
Name:		
Address:		
City:	State:	Zip: